IT SEEMED LIKE
A GOOD IDEA AT
THE TIME

IT SEEMED LIKE A GOOD IDEA AT THE TIME

Maureen Anne Morgan

To order additional copies of this book, contact:
Xlibris
AU TFN: 1 800 844 927 (Toll Free inside Australia)
AU Local: (02) 8310 8187 (+61 2 8310 8187 from outside Australia)
www.Xlibris.com.au
Orders@Xlibris.com.au
841162

CONTENTS

CHAPTER 1

2008 — It's Too Late When They Die

SLUMPED ON MY MOTHER'S bed, eyes brimming with tears, I gazed at the green velvet pouch in my hand. Inside was a gold ring and an Australian Commonwealth Military Forces badge, love tokens given to my mother by my father more than sixty-seven years ago. Wrapping my arms around myself, overwhelmed with grief and remorse, I started to sob uncontrollably as realisation dawned. My mother had kept these trinkets so that if ever I endeavoured to find my father, I would have proof that I was his daughter, but all through her lifetime, I hadn't been interested. As a small child, I had been given a photograph of my father with his full name. At seven, I had been brought from London to Sydney, his home city, and had lived here ever since, without ever bothering to find him. I realised now that I had cocooned myself in dreams of a fantasy father and knew, deep in my heart, no mere mortal could compete with that.

Why hadn't I had a real conversation with my mother about my birth? Now it was too late. As I grew older, I was always in the moment of living, never looking at the past. Therefore, I had scorned my younger sister's interest in genealogy, ignored my doctor's requests for information about family history of disease and even discounted my daughter-in-law's suggestion 'You really should write your story'.

How I regretted not asking questions, not taking steps to find out; now it was too late. That night, I wrote my mother's eulogy, which announced to my unsuspecting siblings that she had had a previous love and I was, in fact, their half-sister.

So I too joined Ancestry.com and discovered that I came from a long line of strong, resolute women. Starting with my maternal great-grandmother, Elizabeth Emma Coombs, whose first three girls were born, baptised and buried before they reached their second birthday. Elizabeth persevered, having three more girls and two sons. The First World War claimed her husband, her younger son and her two brothers. Still, she battled on, helping her oldest daughter, Grace, my grandmother, look after her three-year-old daughter while my grandfather was at war. Finally, in the 1930s, Elizabeth took her two younger daughters, Charlotte and Annie, and emigrated to Australia.

Judging from her photograph, my grandmother Grace grew to be a beautiful young lady and a fur finisher by trade. From knowing her in later life, she was obviously cultured, loving reading, classical music, opera, theatre and ballroom dancing. She was neat and tidy, always putting everything in its place. In the day, she loved to cook and at night was always working on crochet or knitting and listening to music.

In 1912, Grace met and fell in love with Ralph Buckland Wood, a man older by eight years. One thing led to another, and on 5 January 1913, they were married in Lambeth, a suburb of London. Six months later, on 19 July 1913, Irene Edith Gertrude Wood (called Rene) was born.

In 1914, World War 1 began, and Ralph enlisted. Grace, with Rene, moved back to her parents. My paternal great-grandmother Sarah died in 1916. The following year, her son Ralph, my grandfather, was invalided out of the war. He and his wife moved in with his father. In 1918, the twins arrived, John Charles Stanley and Joan Grace Charlotte, my mother.

Four years later, on 23 April 1922, another boy was born, Ronald Stanley Ralph (called Bun). Irene never returned home to her real parents, so my mother grew up as the only girl with two boisterous brothers.

Joan proved to be a real tomboy. At fourteen, she was smoking tobacco rolled in newspaper and swigging rum with her brothers. So dismayed was my grandmother with her out-of-control daughter that she sent her, aged fifteen, to board at a convent. It was there that my mother learnt to care for orphaned children, which led her to train as a nurse at King's College Hospital in London. When war began in

1939, my mother was transferred to Colchester Hospital as bombing casualties were expected in a port city with an army base nearby.

Her two brothers who had joined the navy were on different ships, so it was an anxious time for the family listening to shipping reports. Both Great-Grandfather and Grandfather stayed at home, but Grandmother became an air raid warden, donning her uniform and guiding people to public shelters.

In 1941, my mother met and fell in love with a patient, an Australian soldier, Reginald William James Johnston, a man ten years her senior. He loved horses, and his idea of a date was to come to London to see Buckingham Palace and visit the stables.

One thing led to another, and when the Battle of Britain was at its height, my mum discovered she was pregnant. Reg had already rejoined the war, so Mum couldn't tell him the news. Being a nurse, she could possibly have found a way to terminate the pregnancy but decided to come home and tell her family.

Father was ready to show her the door (forgetting he had once been in a similar situation). Mother said,

'Come home and I will look after the baby while you go to work'.

Brothers said, 'Make the guy marry you now so you will be looked after by the Australian government'.

Brother Jack travelled to Colchester to tell Reg face to face but found he had already left for the Middle East. A senior officer told Jack that Reg already had a wife at home, and although he may be very fond of Joan, he was unable to marry.

Mum worked until the end of October, and I was born in Colchester Hospital on 18 November 1941.

As soon as I could understand, my mother told me that my father was an Australian soldier who had gone to fight in the war. As he didn't come back, I assumed he had died fighting for his country. Many children in my class at school had lost their fathers, so I was not alone. My mother also gave me a photo of my father and his full name if ever I wanted to find any relatives. To my regret, I was never interested while my mother was alive. It was only after her death that I bothered to consult Ancestry.com.au and discovered that my father's death certificate dated 1980 was marked childless. I had lived in the same city as he did for over thirty years and never tried to find him. Not only that, but his father and brother had lived in Dee Why, so it was possible that I had taught a relative as I had taught at both Narrabeen and Manly high schools.

Mum and I came back to London in the middle of the blitz. Bombing raids were nearly every night. We had our own air raid shelter in the backyard, which we shared with close neighbours. Mum went to work at the nearby hospital in the morning, and Nana would look after me. When Mum came home, Nana would do the evening shift as air raid warden, coming home late at night, sometimes not until morning.

The home shelter was dark, dank and musty, and rats found a home there as well. One evening, my mother stretched her arm over me and was bitten by a rat. She couldn't do anything about it until the all-clear sounded and we could re-enter the house.

I was a problem for my mother from birth. I had a condition known as ichthyosis, literally 'fish skin', possibly a result of poor prenatal diet, but it meant I screamed when put into a bath or even just washed with water. It must have been very painful. The skin on my hands and legs would split open and bleed, particularly in cold weather, so I had to be wiped with oil instead of being washed. Initially, I couldn't have my hair washed at all, just brushed. I probably was not a sweet-smelling baby.

London was badly bombed in 1943 and 1944, and my mother tried desperately to send me somewhere safe. Children were being sent out of London to the country, but not babies and certainly not babies with a skin condition. Aunt Lottie, who had come to Australia with her mother and sister Annie in 1923, volunteered to sponsor us to come to live with her family in Sydney. My mother couldn't go because nurses were needed and I was too young to travel alone. Nana couldn't leave her ailing husband and was worried about her sons, so we stayed and weathered the bombing.

Doodlebugs or Giddy Bombs

I remember listening for the sound of the giddy bombs, a whirring, screaming high-pitch noise and then sudden silence. You had to run to the air-raid shelter before the sound stopped, or you could be blown to bits.

Inside the shelter, it was safe, but not safe. There was a damp, musty smell and a scary scrabbling sound, rats?

So dark, eyes strained to see. I snuggled into Nan. She spoke to the neighbours.

'Let start singing'.

'Pack up your troubles in your old kit bag and smile, smile, smile'.

One morning, as I walked with Nana to the shop, I could see the school I wanted to go to as a whole block of houses had been flattened by bombs, making the street behind now in full view. I wanted to take a shortcut through the rubble and received a stern lecture on how dangerous bomb sites are, how there could be a bomb in there ready to go off, if you accidentally stepped on it.

My recollections of those war years were everyone dressed in uniform and I couldn't wait to get my school uniform. Food was kept behind the counter, not on open display, but the shopkeeper would give me a sweet, which was a special treat. I learned to listen for the giddy bombs that made a whirring noise, and when that noise stopped, you had to be in the shelter really quickly. I always wanted to have our cat Jinx in the shelter with me as I was frightened of the rats.

Two important events happened during the war years. My great-grandfather died, and I wasn't allowed to go to the funeral, even though I had dressed myself in my best red coat. The funeral party left from our house, and Nana and Grandad with the black wonkles (my childhood name for moustache) walked behind the coffin, while Mum stayed at home with me.

My favourite uncle Bun married, and I was allowed to go to the wedding (in my red coat). Growing up fatherless in war-torn London and being the only child in a house full of adults, I guess I would have been rather spoilt. My favourite relative was Uncle Bun. He was a big bear of a man who filled the doorway when he arrived. With a deep booming voice and big strong hands, he would swing me high in the air, settle me on his shoulders and gallop around the room, finally throwing me on the bed, nuzzling my neck with his prickly whiskers and tickling me until I screamed for mercy. Then he would take me to buy fish and chips for dinner. His nickname for me was Chips because he said I ate so many, I would grow up to look like one.

I guess there was fear in being thrown so high and laughing until I couldn't catch my breath, but that fear was fun. As a sailor, Uncle Bun only lived at home when he was on leave. I utterly adored him and was sad when he had to return to his ship. He had a girlfriend Jo, who was also fun to be around.

Great news, Bun and Jo were to be married, and I was to be flower girl and carry a bouquet! In the weeks that followed this news, as Uncle Bun talked about moving his things from our house to Jo's, a dark threatening thought invaded my mind.

Would he still come and visit me when he was married? When I thought about this, I felt sick in my stomach. My other uncle, Jack, was already married with a baby boy, Michael, and a puppy, which I adored. Mum said our cat, Jinx, would be unhappy and would leave home if we had a dog, so I just pretended my stuffed dog was real. Uncle Jack only came on special occasions, and his family was the centre of his attention, not me.

The unmentionable fear of losing the special relationship with a special uncle caused a dramatic change in my behaviour. Mum said I was being difficult, and I couldn't understand why. In the wedding photos, there is a very serious, rather sad little flower girl with the face of the girl he left behind.

Then the war finally ended. I can still remember the end-of-war street party, with more food than I had ever seen in my life put out on trestle tables in the street and everyone singing and dancing.

Post-war life was so good. I went to dance classes, tap and ballet, which I loved and was happy to practise every day and perform for anyone who would stop and watch.

I learned to play the piano accordion. It must have been a small one, and even then, I could barely get my arms around it. I only learned to use three base buttons, and they had wax glued on to them in three different heights so I could tell which one to press.

I loved dancing class, and afterwards, we would go and buy fish and chips for tea.

At Xmas time, there was the dance class party and concert where I had a star turn as a fairy. Another special treat was going to a pantomime at the Windmill Theatre.

In the summer, we went to Margate Beach and Brighton Pier, and now I could go into the water. I didn't really like it very much, too cold and too rough, and if the wind came up, my legs would crack and bleed again. Hence, I didn't learn to swim.

At last, I started school. The bombed houses had been cleared, but we still had to walk the long way around the block as it was now a construction site. I loved books and reading and was unhappy when I had to give the schoolbooks back, so Nan started my very own bookshelf.

Suddenly, money became important to me. At age five, I received fivepence pocket money if I kept my belongings tidy, and I discovered I could buy sweets and cakes with it. Throughout the war years, one needed coupons and money to buy food and didn't see tempting arrays of edibles on sale. After the war, our local bakery had a wonderful display of cakes in the window. Passing this store on the way to school, breathing in the delicious smell of freshly baked goods, I would try to decide which tempting treat I would buy. A bun for one penny, a cupcake for threepence, but what I really longed for was a cream cake costing sixpence. I was not naturally tidy, so often my gain was less than fivepence. Neither was I a saver; my money burned a hole in my pocket as I gazed at the mouth-watering treats.

Suddenly an idea! Coming home from school, via the bakery, I took Nana's apron from behind the door in the kitchen, a duster and a feather duster from the cupboard and went to my mother's dresser for a scarf. Then doubling the apron around my waist and tying the scarf around my head, I went upstairs to the room of our lodger, Miss Ivy, knocked on the door and asked her if she needed a cleaning lady,

'To dust your furniture for one penny'.

Miss Ivy was a lovely, rather elderly, retired schoolteacher, and she agreed to let me dust the legs of the dining room furniture as she had difficulty getting down. *Such huge furniture, however did she get it upstairs?* I wondered. Interesting smells in her room, lavender maybe, and a strange yellow wood inlay in a chest that smelt slightly exotic.

Emboldened by this success, I ventured next door, and the lady there was happy for me to dust under the furniture in the sitting room as long as I didn't touch anything else. Unfortunately, this neighbour told my mum, who was horrified, and that was the end of my cleaning career. We also found a different way to walk to and from school, avoiding the bakery.

How does this episode show the makings of me? Firstly, what I was then and am now is not only being particularly tidy, having a sweet tooth and a liking for cakes and having a need for immediate satisfaction, unable to wait and save for a week, but also having an enterprising spirit to devise a plan and carry it out secretly when I thought my mother would probably not think it to be a good idea.

CHAPTER 2

1948 – Off to Australia

EARLY DAYS AT SCHOOL I discovered boys played differently from girls. I didn't have any cousins my age, and there were no children of any age living in our part of the street. At school, the boys liked playing chasings, and I preferred to play with them rather than with the girls. Both Mum and Nan knew what happens to girls who liked playing with boys, so my second year started at St Catherine's Catholic School for girls.

Fortunately, this was the year we were selected to go to Australia. Aunt Charlotte (Lottie) sponsored us, providing accommodation, and we became ten pound poms.

I vividly remember packing for the trip. I wanted to take every toy, every book and all my dolls, and why couldn't Jinx the cat go to Australia too?

Thank goodness it had been the *Puss in Boots* pantomime the previous Xmas, and Nan said Jinx wanted to stay in London, as all cats did, and she would look after him for me. I remember my last dance class, saying goodbye to my best friend Pat. My special friend Alan gave me a kiss and said he would come to Australia when he grew up and would find me and marry me.

Mum and I travelled, first by train to Glasgow, and I carried my three favourite dolls as they wouldn't fit in the suitcase. Then we boarded the ship, the 'Empire Brent'. There were so many people on the dock saying goodbye. We didn't have anyone to say goodbye to; Nan was back in London. So we watched everyone else, waving, crying and throwing streamers. I thought that was a bit silly; streamers were for parties and Xmas, not for a big adventure on a boat. I wondered why so many people were crying; for me, it was a happy day, and it was for my mum. I think she may have thought

9

she would find my dad in Australia, and she did, but in a way she hadn't expected.

The ship was so huge; Mum and I kept getting lost, finding our way to the dining room and to the deck we were assigned to go for lifeboat drill. This happened every morning. At the sound of a long-drawn-out siren, you had to run to your cabin, grab your life jacket and then hurry to your deck for roll call. With everyone on the ship all scurrying somewhere, it was chaos, but we managed to arrive, fit our life jackets and answer our names. I was somewhat disappointed we didn't practise getting into the lifeboats, and by the time the six-week voyage was over, I was heartily sick of the drill. Mum and I shared a cabin with a lady with two girls a little older than me. There wasn't much to do on the ship, not like cruise ships today, but sometimes a crew member would organise deck games for adults and children.

I remember three exciting events that happened during that voyage.

The first was after many days of travelling, the ship ceased her eternal motion. She had docked at Port Said, somewhere in the middle of the world. The sky was blue, the heat so intense, there seemed to be a shimmer from the impressive white building that dominated the port. It must surely be a city as the maze of buildings stretched as far as the eye could see. For a child used to London's grey stone buildings, these were all in brown or dazzling white. It seemed to be a magical place.

We were on the sea, but there was no smell of the sea, just a warm, sweet, spicy smell from the land. I was amazed at the sight of so many African and Middle Eastern people, all wearing long flowing robes, even over their heads. Remember, at the end of the war, our part of London had very few non-English people, not like now when Brixton has more black than white residents. The atmosphere was electric, the sounds unfamiliar and exciting. I was so disappointed that we could not get off and explore further as some passengers did, but the ten pound poms were not allowed ashore. Deep in my soul, a resolution was made: One day, when I was an adult, I would get off a ship in a strange, exotic land and go and explore.

Enterprising hawkers in small boats surrounded our ship, calling out in broken English and holding up their wares. If someone wanted to buy, a crewman would swing a basket down to the seller and then haul up the purchase for inspection. If you agreed to buy, you put your money (English pounds) in the basket and kept the goods. The lady in our cabin bought a leather bag, and Mum did too, and it was a treasured possession right up till her death. I wanted to buy a little bird as one of the boats was full of unusual livestock, birds in cages and also free, running around loose in the boat. We didn't know about Australia's strict quarantine laws, but luckily, my mother said I could get a bird in Australia as it would be happier in its own country.

The second big event, after we passed through the Suez Canal, was the crossing of the line. I couldn't understand what the fuss was all about; Mum said we were at the equator, so we would be on the other side of the world from England.

I thought maybe it would be like climbing a sea wall and then shooting down the other side, but no, we seemed to be stationary, on a flat sea with brilliant blue sky and a really hot sun, and all the crew went mad. They had dressed up; King Neptune with his trident ruled, and everyone had to jump over a line made with a thick hose while being belted with seaweed and hosed with water. It was good fun actually because it was so hot, you didn't mind getting soaking wet.

The third big event of that long sea voyage was that my mother managed to fall in love with a passenger, Sydney Vinnard, a Welshman bound for South Australia to live with his sister. Mum had introduced me to Taffy, as he was called, early in the voyage and would often leave me with the older girls while she and their mother went for a quiet drink with other adults. I rather enjoyed this adult-free playtime and was totally surprised when, the evening before we arrived in Australia, Mum came in after I had gone to bed, kissed me and said,

'Would you like Taffy to be your daddy?'

I vividly remember looking up into her face, which was so radiant, her eyes shining excitedly, and thought I'd better say yes.

I hadn't given Taffy a thought before. He'd been around a lot, of course, but really hadn't had much to do with me; he didn't play games or even talk to me. I'd never had a dad, only a special uncle who did play games, cuddle and tickle me and give me rides on his shoulders. I really didn't know what a dad did, but if he made my mum so happy, then I guess he'd do.

The following day, we arrived in Freemantle, and there were many white people to greet us, waving flags and yelling. I was surprised they were all white as my schoolbook on Australia had said black people lived there and lots of strange animals.

Mum said a tearful goodbye to Taffy, who had to catch a train to Adelaide and meet his sister. He vowed to follow her to NSW and marry her straight away.

The ship stopped in Port Melbourne, and many people left, including our cabin mates. Then we arrived in Sydney. It was a beautiful blue-sky sunny day, considering it was July and midwinter. When we walked down the gangplank and into the terminal, there was an incredible feast spread out for us. Sandwiches, scones, cupcakes and my first lamington. I thought Australia was heaven!

Aunt Lottie and Uncle Fred met us and drove us home to Punchbowl, where they lived with their three children, Charlie, Kathy and Freddy. Mum and I shared a double bed in the spare room, but I was told I would be sharing Kathy's room as soon as a bed was found for me. Here I must admit that, for all of my nearly seven years, I had always slept with either my mum or my nan, and I was quite nervous about sharing a room with a stranger. Kathy was ten and seemed so much bigger than me, and her brothers were twelve and eight and so noisy and rough.

Kathy proved to be very nice. I think she liked having another girl in the house. She would read me a bedtime story and would walk me to school and back home. I also started Sunday school with the Poole children. They were Baptists, so I became one too.

I was enrolled at Punchbowl Public School, at first in the infants school in second class, but with the new year, I entered primary and had the best teacher in the world, Mr Ridge. He is the only teacher whose name I still remember, from six months in his class, nearly seventy years ago. I adored him; he was everything I thought a dad should be: kind, patient, encouraging and fun to be around.

Everything my new dad was not.

True to his word, Sidney Vinnard found his way to 101 Dudley St Punchbowl, took my mother to the Sydney Registry Office and married her on 17 July 1948.

Then he came back to Aunt Lottie's house to live with us.

Life was never to be the same again.

Not only did I now sleep in a different room to my mother, but also I was not allowed to jump into her bed for a cuddle on a weekend morning. The first time I tried this, a grumpy male voice abruptly ordered me back to my bed, and then I was given a stern lecture on good manners: always knock on a closed door and wait until you are permitted to enter. Mum would tuck me into bed and give me a cuddle then, but otherwise, shows of affection were distinctly frowned upon.

Good manners seemed to rule my life. My table manners were unacceptable to the new power figure in the house. I would be banished to my room at dinner time if I made mistakes, leaving the rest of my dinner and not getting any dessert. The most memorable occasion of this was on Freddie's birthday. He was having my favourite meal, savoury mince followed by birthday cake, and I was banished from the table. That night, I cried myself to sleep, a mixture of self-pity and rage, and I hated my entire family – my mother for marrying this monster, my nana for not coming with me and saving me and my uncle Bun for marrying someone else and not coming to save me.

I think that might have been the first time I dreamt about my fantasy father, a mixture of Uncle Bun and Mr Ridge, who would come and find me and carry me away.

It was 25 December in Australia, and I couldn't believe it was Xmas. True, we made Christmas cards at school, the nativity scene was placed in the church, and carols played on the radio, but it was so hot, you wouldn't want to roast chestnuts and toast marshmallows over a fire. There wasn't even Christmas pudding, just a pudding I had never seen before called pavlova, with strawberries and passionfruit all over it. It was very nice, but I missed looking for threepences in the traditional pudding. Best of all though, Mum had kept her promise, and I had a beautiful Australian blue budgerigar in a cage.

'It is a budgie, and you can teach him to talk,' I was told, but although I tried very hard, he never repeated a word I said to him.

My stay in Punchbowl was important for three reasons:

1. I learned from my classmates that I was a bastard (i.e. illegitimate).

   I was quite proud of this fact because I did not want to be thought of as Mr Vinnard's daughter, and I believed I had a father who was tall, tanned and gentle and smiled all the time. I had a photo to prove it.

   To be fair to my stepfather, he had formerly adopted me at the same time that he married my mother, so I was officially called Vinnard. I believe he treated me in the same way that he treated my as-yet-unborn siblings, his own children. This was the way he was raised; children were to be seen as polite and obedient, and any deviation from this was punished with the strap.

2. I could vent my internal anger against poor Aunt Lottie. She had allowed Mr Vinnard to stay in her house and hadn't objected to his treatment of me.

   This allowed me to bypass blaming my mother, although I did harbour resentment that I had said yes to the question 'Do you want Taffy to be your daddy?'

   To be fair to Aunt Lottie, she gave me the most wonderful experience by taking me with her family to the Royal Easter Show in Moore Park, Sydney. Mum was largely pregnant and not a well lady at this time, her husband stayed home to look after her, and we went by train and tram to the showground. It was the most magical day, more horses, dogs and cows than I had ever seen in my life. The grand parade was amazing, and I made a vow that one day I would participate in that parade. The woodchopping was an eye-opener, and the very last thing we went to was the Hall of Industries, where we each chose a sample bag of lollies to take home. I was in heaven and was determined to go every year.

3. I began my affair with a fantasy father, a mixture of Uncle Bun and Mr Ridge.

More than sixty years later, ancestry.com supplied information about my father. According to the 1949 electoral roll, he and his wife were then living in James St, Punchbowl.

CHAPTER 3

1949 – New Baby, New Home, New School

WHEN, IN LATE 1948, it was obvious that Mum was pregnant, I was thrilled to have a new baby (hoping for a girl). My wish came true, and Margaret Helen was born on 21 April 1949. I was entranced with this small creature and happily became her second mother, taking her for walks in the pram, making her bed, fetching her clothes and nappies and helping to give her a bottle.

Somehow, this enthusiasm lost its lustre by being expected rather than just enjoyed. I remember once being punished for telling lies because I said yes to the question 'Have you made your bed'? My stepfather smacked me for telling lies because even though I had made my own bed, I had not made the baby's bed.

Nevertheless, I adored my little sister.

So now we were a family of four staying in an accommodation offered to two.

The Housing Commission had been approached, and we were offered a place at Hargrave Park emergency housing hostel, so we moved. I was very upset to say goodbye to my teacher and told him I would always remember him. But did I ever try to trace him and send a thank-you card? No!

Hargrave Park had been a camp for army personnel and consisted of corrugated tin huts divided into three, allowing each family two bedrooms, a kitchen and a living space. The bathroom, toilet and laundry in an adjacent block were shared, so when it was raining, we washed in a tub in the kitchen. The huts were not lined, so they were extremely hot in the summer and very cold in the winter. We poms could cope with the chill but found the heat unbearable.

The huts were in rows, with no playing area between. A large oval was nearby, but I wasn't allowed to go as teenage boys played footy and cricket there. Neither could I explore the bushland that formed a barrier on one side as my British parents were afraid of snakes, spiders and other creepy crawlies.

My life revolved around baby Margaret, who was not a very well baby. I spent most of my time pushing her around the row of huts to get her to sleep.

This was where we had our first puppy, a fox terrier called Wendy. Mr Vinnard had a fox terrier when he was young, so that was what we had. Now I learned what a family animal was. I had always owned any animal in the house, including my new bird. Years later, Margaret and I would fight about whose dog Wendy had been.

I started school at Warwick Farm Primary, a walking distance from home, which meant I had the freedom to explore the rest of the camp as long as I made it to school on time. Here I had another male teacher, but totally unlike my previous one. He was tall, dark and thin, never smiled and used the cane frequently on boys and girls.

I had always been a chatterbox. Mr Ridge had made me sit down the front by myself to cure my continual talking. This new teacher relied on caning me in front of the class for persistent chatter. I became a bit of a rebel hero because I was caned as often as the boys and I didn't cry.

Interestingly, I had my new stepfather to thank for that. His idea of punishment was to send you to your room and then come in some time later and give you the strap, preferably on a bare bottom. I discovered my mother did not come in and save me, but then again, she had used a hairbrush on my covered bottom when she put me over her knee. While I waited for my punishment, I willed myself not to cry, just like the brave heroines in books I had read. Of course, I did break down after a few whacks on the bare flesh. But the determination to not cry held me in good stead at school when it was at most three cuts on each hand. I could handle that.

I must have had a reputation in that class. That was the year I had my appendix out, and when I came back to school, I happily showed my scar to anyone who wanted to look, girls and boys. Well, we were caught, and I nearly did cry that time when I was caned. I really couldn't understand what all the fuss was about. None of the others had had an operation like mine, so it was necessary that they see the resulting scar and hear the gruesome details. I didn't understand why the words disgusting, rude and sexual were used against me.

Still, when the school had a mini popularity show and each class chose a queen, I was voted queen of fourth class. I don't know where my beautiful satin dress came from. It looked as if it had been a flower girl's outfit for a much-smaller child as Mum had to attach some netting to the bottom so that I had a floor-length gown. We queens had to collect money for some charity, and the girl who collected the most became queen of the school. She definitely did not come from Hargrave Park emergency housing.

The following year, 1950, Margaret was walking, and Mum was pregnant again. Best of all, Nana made her way to Australia. I was thrilled to have my nana back again and didn't mind sharing her with another baby. We went to Sydney to meet her ship. I was so excited, looking forward to the feast that we had when we arrived. But that welcome feast had been for the war-torn ten pound poms. People paying their own way were not treated to that; they just came off the ship, and that was it.

At the terminal, I met Nana's brother, Uncle Bob, and his wife, Annie. They lived in Dulwich Hill, and Nana was to stay with them until she found a place of her own. Unfortunately, she couldn't stay with us; she just came each week to help Mum with babies and shopping. Later, finding accommodation in the city, Nana took up her cultural life again, doing ballroom dancing and going to the theatre. She had a very good friend whom she had met on the boat and we called Aunt Esther. Aunt Esther had a special friend we called Uncle Eddie. They would sometimes visit us, and we loved seeing them as they were our only people we saw.

Then baby Rosemary arrived on 12 September 1950.

With the arrival of a third child, we climbed higher on the list for a housing commission house, and by Xmas of the following year, we had moved into 14 Clack St Villawood.

A real house, still with two bedrooms, but with an indoor bathroom and laundry, an outside toilet and a big backyard. Milk was delivered in a huge urn on the back of a truck, and I would take a billy out to fill up and then put the milk in the ice chest in the kitchen. Bread was delivered by horse and cart, the horse diligently stopping at each gate while the driver fetched your unsliced loaf, white or brown. The corner store was two blocks away on the main road, next to the local primary school, and the big shops were a bus ride away in Parramatta, where there was also a magnificent cinema, The Roxy. Very elaborate it was, decorated with statues and exotic lights and with an upstairs and downstairs section inside. The first movie I had ever seen was *Peter Pan*, which Nana took me to on my birthday. The following year, it was the even more spectacular *Carmen Jones*.

I made friends with a girl my age, Margaret, who lived across the road from us. She went to the Catholic school in Guildford, and Mum said I could go there too.

When school term started, we were interviewed by the head nun and told I didn't have the necessary qualifications to go to a Catholic school; I hadn't done my first communion. Then although the local public school was walking distance from home, Mum enrolled me at Guildford Public School, a bus ride away. In later years, when a similar situation happened with my sisters, I believe Mum did not want her children to go to school in a housing commission area but found a better suburb to send her kids.

Villawood was where I became totally horse mad. Mum thought maybe I had inherited horse mania from my dad as she told me that while visiting Margate at about three years of age, I wanted a pony ride rather than fairy floss. At our new house, there was a paddock in the street behind us where an aboriginal man tethered two horses, Tommy and Ginger. Every school day, I detoured past the paddock and fed my sandwiches to the horses. I never spoke to their owner. I heard him call their names, and they responded.

I read every horse book available in the school library and started my collection of paper horses, cut from newspaper and magazines.

Every horse was named, given a height, age, colour and breeding and stuck into an old schoolbook. At home, on the weekend, I would pretend I was riding one of them and gallop around the backyard, fast on the thoroughbred, prancing on the Arab, and when I was puffed, I led the yearling around. I can't remember the hideous crime I committed to have my treasured horse pictures confiscated and burned, but I remember the pain of losing them and the hatred I felt at the injustice of it all. My mother realised the depth of my unhappiness at losing my paper horses, so she walked with me to the paddock and took a photo of my favourite horse, Tommy.

Mum tried to turn my interest into something more cultural, and I began piano lessons. I enjoyed this, but of course, there was no possibility of having a piano to practice on, so I really didn't get very far. My piano teacher had another student my age who was a girl guide, and she did a 'bob a job' for the teacher, so I did too. Then when the piano teacher told me she had a friend with a piano who would let me practise if I went to the shop for her, I did that and also did the guides 'bob a job' for her and her neighbour. This way, I started my secret stash, saving up to buy a horse.

A Christian influence was important to my parents, so I started Sunday school at the Church of England in Guildford. As Margaret was now four, she came too, and then I was asked to take the two little boys next door and another little girl, so at the tender age of eleven, I chaperoned two preschoolers and two infant schoolchildren on the bus to Guildford.

The hierarchy at the church thought I had wonderful leadership material and convinced my parents to let me join the Girls' Brigade, which was an after-school activity. I loved this release from childcare and household duties and joined in enthusiastically, singing in the church choir and planning to go carol singing in December. This outing was vetoed when it was revealed we would be going at 7.30 at night and males were included. From my exposure to the church, I developed the philosophy that you could really do what you liked when you were young and then truly repent, become a nun when you were older, and win your pass to paradise.

One transgression I have truly repented was the hurt I caused my treasured sister Margaret. It was my job to bathe her at night. She loved playing in the bath using her Xmas bubble bath to make herself completely soapy and slippery. One night, I was in a hurry; I think I had homework to do. Margaret wasn't ready to stop playing, so I tried to drag her out of the bath, and as she was slippery, I dropped her on the tiled floor, and she split her chin open. She must have been less than two as she did not have the verbal capacity to tell what really happened. I said she had fallen when I was getting her out of the bath (which was strictly speaking true) but not what she would have said had she been capable. I thought my guilty secret would die with me, but only a few years ago, Margaret revealed she had a very vivid memory of that event.

After singing in church, I joined the school choir and sang in the Combined Primary Schools Concert held at Sydney Town Hall. I had never been into the city before. To go there at dusk, when the lights were beginning to glow, was magical. On stage, sitting up high under the organ, looking down at the audience and up at the balcony, I felt so special. Then the orchestra came on stage, and there were so many of them. At school, our practises had been with just a piano. To hear the sound of a full live orchestra for the first time was amazing: blaring brass, swirling strings, clashing cymbals and deafening drums. Most of all, I remember the magnificent sound of the organ, and the deep vibrations pounded right through me and sent shivers up my spine. I can still remember the face of the conductor, a Mr Terrance Hunt, who would open his eyes so wide, mouth the words so clearly, wave his baton so frantically, that we all sang our hearts out for him.

Nana took me into town and back to her flat in the city. That was a magical weekend. We walked home that night, from the gracefully illuminated Town Hall, through the magnificent Hyde Park, past the gushing fountain and majestic St Mary's Cathedral to Nan's Crown St upstairs flat. That night, I slept peacefully, snuggled into Nan and not wakened by a fretful baby. Next day, we had lunch at Repin's Coffee Lounge, and I felt so grown up and sophisticated.

Classical music was not a feature of my home. That was the first time I had heard a full live orchestra, and I was hooked. High school enabled me to go to symphony concerts, and to this day, I love to hear a live orchestra play and a massed choir sing.

CHAPTER 4

1952 – A Tragedy and My First Swimming Lesson

A TRAGIC EVENT HAPPENED one day as I was on my way to Guildford Primary School, which was on the other side of the railway line from where my bus set down. Pedestrians would walk across the tracks at the car crossing. In those days, there were no flashing lights or automation, not even personnel to supervise. A station employee would come down and close the gate with just a slip-over handle and then walk back to collect the tickets. On that fateful day, a crowd of schoolchildren waited, watching the city-bound train leave the station. Suddenly, a rather-large boy opened the gate and, with his younger sister following, started to walk across. The approaching Liverpool train hit him, and he landed face down on the road. The girl was carried up into the space between the train and the station.

On the platform, it would have been chaos, staff rushing to get help, passengers asking what had happened and no doubt a distraught driver trying to explain. But at the crossing, it was as if death had lowered a shroud of silence. A man ran from his car and spread a towel over the boy's body. The gate was open, so the children cautiously made their way over the crossing, staring at the covered form, stunned into silence, their brains endeavouring to compute what their eyes had just seen. No one speaking, no one crying, all in shock and probably with the feeling 'That could have been me. What must it feel like to die?'

Once at school, however, we lost no time telling the office and then all our friends what had happened, including all the gory details, which became gorier as the story spread through the school. At least one person actually knew the two victims, so at our morning assembly,

25

the entire school was told the dreadful news with a stern warning how dangerous the level crossing was. Now we were ordered, under threat of detention, if we were caught using the crossing in future, to walk over the bridge. We had a minute silence while we thought of the two dead children and how silly they had been.

The following day, a railways employee placed a padlock on each gate, and people at the crossing had to wait until he came back to open it. Apart from a report in the paper, nothing more was said about the matter. I left that school at the end of that year, and that system was still in place.

How different it would be today if a similar situation happened. Parents rushing for counsellors and lawyers, shocked jocks on radios raging about governmental neglect and teachers made to patrol the station, making sure their pupils crossed in the correct manner.

My stepfather then worked for the railway, and I had the same lecture at home about how level crossings were so dangerous. I dared not reveal I had used that method of crossing the line all year. Automation did not come until 1982, some three decades later.

The good thing about my stepfather's job was that we went to the railway Xmas picnic each year. It was a long way to Clifton Gardens, by bus, train, bus, but Nan came too, and there was free ice cream, lollies and a present for each child. This was our once-a-year trip to a swimming area, and in the warmth of an Australian climate, my skin problem was much better. However, I still had not learned to swim. At Warwick Farm School, I had brought home a form for free government swimming lessons to be held at Liverpool Swim Centre, but Mum was too busy with her baby and her own health problems to take me, and I wasn't allowed to go on my own. Then in sixth class at Guildford Primary, lessons were offered at Parramatta Pool, and once again, it was not considered an important thing to do. As we only went near water once a year, it didn't seem important to me either.

I had pestered Mum to go to the Easter Show every year since the year Aunt Lottie had taken me. Finally, with Rosemary in a stroller and Margaret walking, holding Nan's hand, we went on Children's Day, when the show bags were said to be sold cheaper. Once again, I watched the Grand Parade and vowed to be a part, particularly ogling the Arabs, my horse of preference. This time, I also watched show jumping as there was room on the grassy sides of the main ring to sit and eat the sandwiches we had brought. Another silent promise was made: One day, I would ride a horse over jumps.

We must have been fairly affluent that year, as in the January holidays, we made the long voyage to Manly. It was a warm summer day when we set out, carrying towels, sandwiches and bottles of made-up cordial. First a bus, then a train, and then a bus again until finally we reached Circular Quay and the South Steyne ferry. This time, not only Nana, but also Aunt Esther and Uncle Eddie came too, meeting us at the wharf.

I thought the ferry was rather small compared with the Empire Brent, but I loved watching the engine throb and turn, and I savoured the smell of oil and diesoline. The ride was quite sedate until we hit the heads. Then I remembered the rolling motion that made me feel quite nauseous, and the sight of the water rising fuelled fear within me.

Arriving at Manly wharf, most of the crowd went straight ahead up The Corso, and I longed to see where they were going, but we made a sharp left turn and proceeded to Manly Harbour Pool. In the fifties, the pool was quite impressive, with a walkway at the shark net side, featuring giant slippery dips and a pontoon in the middle.

The water seemed to be filled with children, and the sand was covered with people. At the far end was a very imposing building, which I learned was the changing rooms.

This was my first visit to an Australian beach, and in my entire life, I had only visited a beach four times. In addition, I had been born with a skin complaint, ichthyosis, which dictated that I could not be washed in water for the first twelve months.

Consequently, I was rather nervous in any water, particularly the moving kind. I held my four-year-old sister's hand and paddled in the shallows. Then I sat down, letting the cold-water waves wash over my legs while my feet disappeared in the sand. Uncle Eddie, who had come to Australia as a young man and raised children in the Australian fashion of plenty of sun, sand and swimming, decided I should learn to swim. Taking my hand, he coaxed me into deeper water (actually about waist high), and when the ferry arrived, creating turbulence, he said, 'Try jumping the waves'.

I couldn't lift both feet together as I didn't like the way the sand kept shifting underneath them. The waves felt icy when other children my age dashed past me, splashing me. I decided to turn back when my uncle grabbed my other hand and pulled me, causing me to stumble and fall, dreaded cold water over my head, up my nose and in my mouth when I squealed. I stumbled on shifting sands, flailing my arms, unable to get upright. Another wave knocked me down, fighting off Uncle's attempts to help. Heart thumping, I tried to crawl out of the water. Finally, I made it, refusing ever to go back into moving sand and water again. Unhappy and humiliated, I spent the rest of the day lying face down, wishing I could disappear into the hated sand, and as a result became badly sunburnt. Mum worried that my skin condition might be worsened in the water. Stepfather was not impressed with an adult male handling his eleven-year-old ward, so I didn't get very far with my one and only swimming lesson.

About lunchtime, Uncle Eddie took me to the imposing building, where there was a kiosk selling potato scallops and boiling water for adults to make a cup of tea. This would become my job every time we came to Manly, and in a strange quirk of fate, among those noisy young men serving was the man who would one day become my husband.

Eddie and Esther never came to Manly with us again, but we visited annually. I finally learnt to swim some sixteen years later in a heated tiled pool, where I had taken my toddler to be drown-proofed.

CHAPTER 5

1953 – Off to High School and the Start of Wanderlust

IN 1953, MUM WAS pregnant again, and on 12 August, Owen, the long-awaited son, arrived. It had been a difficult pregnancy, and I had many days away from school helping out when Mum had to go to the hospital. I was relieved when the baby was born, especially as now we had a boy in the family, so surely Mum wouldn't be pregnant again.

At the end of 1953, I had to select my high school. The local school for Guildford area was Parramatta High, the only coed school in Sydney. My parents didn't want me ensconced with testosterone-fuelled teenage boys. Those wanting an all-girls school could send their daughters to Auburn Home Science, but this school did not teach matriculation subjects and terminated at intermediate level. My mother had greater ambitions for me. That was how I came to be enrolled at Burwood Girls High. I received my acceptance before the term ended, and my best friend said she would ask her mother to apply for her to go there as well.

The most exciting thing, though, was now I had a student transport pass. To get to Burwood from home meant a bus ride to either Granville or Chester Hill station and then a train ride of at least six stops from there. Having experimented with different ways of getting to school and armed with bus timetables for each option, I then branched out beyond Burwood. I could visit my friends at their houses in Lewisham, or Haberfield, going home with them on the school bus and then finding my way to the train station and Villawood. I exaggerated end-of-class times, joined non-existent clubs like drama or choir to extend my estimated time of arrival home, left earlier than needed to stop at stations beyond Burwood and said I had my nose in a book and was carried on. I went home with everyone I knew who caught a school bus just to look at the route and then find my way back, saying I had got on the wrong bus by mistake. In this way, I discovered other non-housing commission neighbourhoods with beautiful or historic houses and interesting streets.

By the time I had finished first form, I had ridden every train line out from Strathfield and every school bus out from Burwood High.

I loved school, worked hard and got good grades. The uniform code seemed a bit silly and far too expensive. Absolutely essential were hats, felt for winter and panama for summer; tunic and shirt, long sleeve in winter and short sleeve in summer, worn with tie, blazer and gloves, all year round; and black shoes with stockings in winter and socks in summer. There was no uniform shop, so Mum had to lay-by the winter gear, while I wore a tunic that hopefully would last five years by being taken up and let down annually. My shoes were from a disposal store and were never very comfortable, and I hated the hat and gloves, worried that I would lose them, knowing how expensive they had been.

I must give my mother credit for managing to feed and clothe her growing family on what must have been a minimum wage. She made all our dresses and, together with Nana, knitted all our woollens. Christmas stocking presents were new school supplies, new toothbrush or hairbrush, maybe fancy clips, and definitely a colouring and reading book. Each year, one child would get a favourite toy; we waited for it to be our turn. Birthday present was a new piece of clothing, pyjamas or undies, etc.

So while I hated my uniform, I took good care of it because I knew what a struggle the purchase was for my mum. Also, I was grateful to it for camouflage purposes. In my uniform, complete with hat and gloves, I could have been a private school pupil travelling long distances to get home from extra curriculum activities. I was never questioned travelling by train or bus.

A fleeting moment which was to become a significant lifetime memory happened in second form, one practical home science lesson. The class had finished, and we were waiting for the bell to ring when I repositioned the sloping canisters into the correct order. Just then, the head of the department walked past and asked,

'Who straightened the canisters?'

Somewhat shame faced, I admitted I had, and she replied,

'Thank you, dear, you have a tidy eye'.

I was dumbfounded. No one had ever said I was a tidy child; quite the opposite, I was always being berated for leaving things lying about and being generally scatty. That compliment stayed with me, and some ten years later when I was teaching at Rooty Hill High and that same teacher was head mistress at St Mary's High, I was able to tell her how much that praise had meant to me. She remembered the incident and laughingly said she recalled a very untidy girl unconsciously doing a tidy deed and felt that should be rewarded.

CHAPTER 6

1954 – Horses Lead Me Down the Wrong Path

HORSE MANIA HAD NOT subsided in this new school environment. I wanted to wear a ponytail, which was against the school rules in this age of the bodgie and widgie. If ever I heard the clip-clop of hooves, even if it was just the baker's cart, I could not resist rising to look out of the window. Once late in the year in first form, we had a practise teacher who asked us to hand in some work. I wrote my name as Winnie Stable. The whole class roared with laughter when she read out the name; everyone knew who it was. Fortunately, she just laughed, but my classroom teacher was not amused, and that afternoon, I couldn't roam as I really was in detention. I remember checking the time and resolving to use that as an excuse some other time.

These two passions, horses and seeing new sights, came together one morning in second form when, on the train going to school, I saw three horses (two bays and a chestnut) running free just before the train pulled into Flemington station. Without a second thought, I was off the train and in pursuit. By the time I reached the place where I had viewed them, they had vanished, and only empty streets surrounded me.

But this was the Flemington saleyards, where trains arrived loaded with sheep and cattle en route to the Flemington Abattoir. There were dogs hunting animals out of the train trucks and men on horses driving the cattle off to where I didn't know. I rushed over to open a gate for one group, and the rider waved and thanked me, saying, 'Make sure you shut it after me'.

All thought of school disappeared. It was too late to get there now, so I stayed, opening gates, patting horses until all the cattle had left, and there was just one old man with a horse and cart and three dogs, unloading the sheep. He offered me a ride in the cart if I would open gates for him on the way to the shearing sheds. So without a second thought, I climbed in. I watched the dogs in amazement as they kept the flock together and, moving at a steady pace, proceeded out of the railway area and down a long track to the shearing shed, just before Parramatta Road. Then I helped open gates while the dogs separated the sheep into two groups in different yards.

The bossman of the shearing shed offered to show me a shearer in action, so I entered the shed, smelling the rich mixture of oil, tar, urine and sweat. It was another world, and I was mesmerised. I watched the speed of the shearer, winced when he drew blood and saw the boy rush in with the tar brush and then pick up the shorn fleece and stuff it into a huge bag.

Then the old man said, 'I'm off home for lunch. Do you want to come and help unharness the horse?' Did I ever? A dream came true. So off we went to one of the houses backing on to the saleyards area. True to his word, he showed me how to remove the cart and harness but left the bridle on after unbuckling the long reins.

'Do you want to have a little ride? It will have to be bareback as I don't have a saddle'.

I was in heaven. I scrambled onto the old bay mare's back and just patted her and beamed. The owner tied a piece of rope to use as reins and showed me how to steer. Then I walked the old girl around the yard. My heart was singing; riding a real horse, I wished my real father could see me now! Then I brushed her, gave her the sandwiches and apple from my school bag and was ready to leave when the old man invited me in for a drink.

Now I had had the stranger danger warning; Mum insisted no man was to be trusted. But this was a nice old man whom I had helped and who had let me ride his horse. Now he was offering me a drink, and yes, I was really thirsty.

So in I went, and he gave me a fizzy drink (something we only had at Christmastime) and a cream biscuit (something we never had), and when he stroked my arm and gave me a squeeze, it actually felt nice, as if he were grateful for my help and company. He didn't try to kiss or fondle me, and I felt quite safe in his house. Then it was really time to go home as I wasn't sure how frequently the trains ran from Flemington; I had only travelled beyond Burwood, not before it.

When I made my farewell, the old man said, 'Sheep arrival days are Wednesdays and Thursdays, so if ever you have that day off school and would like to come to help and have a ride, I'll be here'.

What a suggestion to put to a horse-mad girl who could only aim at patting a horse!

I was not averse to taking the odd day off school and had been easily able to catch up on work missed. With my mother's frequent pregnancies and health problems, I had been required to take several odd days off to help her mind a sick child or mind the well one while she took the sick one to a doctor. I knew the wording of the absence note by heart and could easily forge my mother's signature. This was the first time I had forged an absence note, and it was accepted without question.

Unfortunately, I couldn't take off a day a week, but sports day was Wednesday; how could I contrive to be needed at home every Wednesday? I wasn't particularly fond of school sports, softball and netball, and would much rather take horse riding as a sport, so I pondered on the problem for some weeks.

Then fate stepped in, or so it seemed. My mother was diagnosed with breast cancer and had to go for treatment at Camperdown Hospital. The word 'cancer' was never mentioned in our house, as if by avoiding the word, you could avoid the disease. Mum was said to have a problem with her breast, and I had to take a number of days off when she went to the hospital. Nan came to look after us when Mum had her operation, but then miraculously, she was in remission and just on medication. Now was the time to strike and indicate I would be needed to help at home and sports afternoon was the better time for me to miss school and not fall behind in schoolwork.

It worked! Remember we didn't have a telephone and Mum never went to parent-teacher nights (I can't remember if they even had such things then). The staff knew we were migrants without family to assist. They knew about my younger siblings and how my assistance was needed, and the latest notes mentioned Mum going to the hospital.

The staff were very sympathetic, and every Wednesday, I left school at lunchtime, caught the train to Flemington and had a ride on a real horse. The old man with the sheep dogs (I can't even remember his name or that of his horse, just a bay mare) always treated me well, but his fondness and cuddling behaviour intensified. I didn't wear a bra at this age, and he would slide his hand under my shirt, but I would wriggle away and say I don't like that. He would kiss the top of my head, but not my the face. Strangely, I always felt in control of the situation. I only had to say no and he would stop. My riding improved, so I could trot bareback, but the old mare didn't canter.

Every time we went to the shearing shed, the bossman would talk to me, and I told him I was saving up to buy a horse. He told me I could work for him as a rouseabout and that he had a young mare, a pacer who had been badly malnourished, and he was feeding her up. I could play with her and try riding her bareback.

So I left driving the sheep and began to work at the shearing shed. I left the old cart mare and began playing with the two-year-old pacing mare, who didn't have a name, so I called her Gypsy.

I adored the new horse I played with, brushing, feeding, handling and eventually bagging and climbing on. The horse hadn't been broken for riding, only sulky, so I was the first one to actually sit on her and walk her round the yard. I was breaking in a filly when I hadn't even cantered! But we had a bond, and she didn't mind me riding her about. When I tried to trot, she would pace; that is what she was bred to do, but it really wasn't comfortable, so it only happened when she decided to hurry.

I was fourteen when I joined the Shearers' Union to be able to work in a shed during the school holidays. Still playing on the myth that the school was encouraging me to aim at studying vet science at university, I told Mum that a teacher had organised for me to work at the shearing shed at Flemington to give me a wider experience with animals. The following school holiday, I worked two days a week at the shearing shed, earning the princely sum of three pounds per day. Compared with the one pound eight shillings paid at Woolworths, it was a fortune. I had done a deal with the bossman to keep half my wage to put towards the twenty-pound cost of Gypsy, so I really believed I owned her, just had a lay-by for her, which was how I knew Mum bought all our clothes and presents.

Now as my official employer, Jim, the shearing shed manager, drove me home and met my nana, who was staying over. He invited her out for a drink, and this became a regular event: driving me home, then taking Nana out and driving her home to town. Thus, Mum thought he was interested in Nan, not me, and to Nan, he told how hard I worked and how I loved his horse and had a lay-by on it, so Nan conveyed the story of my horse purchase to my mum.

Then came the day I had paid twenty pounds and happily rode Gypsy home from Flemington to Villawood. I had to look up a street directory, avoid Parramatta Road and other main roads and find my way home. It took me nearly two hours. All the family loved Gypsy, even though she would almost walk into the house if she thought you had bread for her.

Like the Aboriginal man, I tethered her where she could get good grass and bought carrots and apples for her. It seemed as if all the neighbours wanted her in their yards to eat the grass and also to supply fertiliser for their gardens.

Can you remember falling passionately in love for the first time? Thinking, hoping, praying that the object of your affection loved you too, walking around in a daze with a perpetual smile on your face and hugging yourself at night, still unable to believe what you had dreamed about had really come true.

That was me in the weeks and months after Gypsy became mine. I went to sleep to the sound of her clomping about the backyard. I woke at daybreak to ride her to the paddock of the day, complete with rope, stake and hammer in a bucket which I would fill at the closest tap. I was home early from school to take Gypsy to canvas the neighbourhood for anyone who would like a quiet horse to eat their grass at night or buy the manure instead. I would take my six-year-old sister with me on these expeditions, proving how gentle this horse was. Saturdays was the best day of all. Riding up to the dairy to meet with other horse riders, swapping notes about good places to ride.

Sunday was the dark day of the week. I was not allowed to do commerce on the Lord's Day. What a waste! In the morning, I took both my sisters and sometimes a neighbour's five-year-old on the bus to Guildford to Sunday school. Once I had loved travelling by bus; now it was just a chore. Then we went back home to the Sunday roast, which took the rest of the morning preparing and half the afternoon cleaning up afterwards. It seemed to be nearly dark by the time I could ride Gypsy.

When my sales of manure had reached a peak, Bobby, the boy from the dairy and grey horse, suggested that as Gypsy was a trotter, I could harness her to the old cart that they had used in years gone by and was now rotting away in a shed.

On investigation, it seemed the tray of the cart was in reasonable condition, as were the shafts. The wheels looked rather worse for wear but still held up. The driver's seat was a very wonky board held in place by a couple of nails and tended to move about, but that didn't seem to be a problem to me. The harness was very dry and stiff and the bridle unusable as the bit was rusted and reins non-existent. All in all, it was a distinct possibility, enabling me to canvas sales further afield. So I rode Gypsy to the dairy, and she was as good at being harnessed as she was at being bridled.

Rope would do for reins, and if I sat carefully on the wonky board, it was okay. I covered two blocks before I had to return and made three prospective sales. This became my working afternoon, harnessing, delivering, and chasing sales. There was a driving need for sales now as Gypsy would need shoes to be able to continue the on-road work. My little sister wanted to come too, and as she was an important factor in the sympathy vote, I agreed.

Then I heard from another rider that the fourth Sunday of each month was Gymkhana Day at Fairfield Showground and everyone with a horse went.

Suddenly an idea! What if I took my sisters to Sunday school by horse and cart? Would there be time for me to get to the gymkhana just for a look and get back in time to take them home? Margaret, a seven-year-old now, was keen, but Rosemary, the five-year-old, was very nervous. She was scared when Gypsy came to her asking to be fed; she had refused to have a ride on her back and had to be held to reluctantly stroke the horse. I had to bribe her by saying I would buy lollies with our bus money.

The fourth Sunday of the month, I took Gypsy to the dairy and harnessed her. Bobby would drive her to the main road and lead his pony behind the cart, while, in our Sunday best, my sisters and I walked to the bus stop. A short pause to buy two lollies and my sisters were bundled into the cart. Quick instructions about how to find the showground and I was off driving my pacer along Woodville Road.

Fortunately, there was not much traffic in those days, and the journey was uneventful until we turned off the main road onto a road that crossed the pipeline and led to the street of our church.

From out of the blue roared a motorbike with two teenage boys laughing and yelling at me. This was too much for Gypsy, who bolted, not at a pace, but a gallop. I frantically tried to slow her and turn her as I thought we were headed back to the main road. But she had other ideas. For months, we had only ridden on the gassy verge, so she swerved and headed onto the footpath. The first big jolt as the cart bounced up the curb found me flying off backwards and hitting my head with a crack on the road. Sitting up, I saw the cart with two screaming children disappearing in the distance, and that was all I remembered until a lady was asking me where I lived.

Fortunately, someone along that footpath, where the horse, cart and passengers were travelling, had left their gate open. Gypsy had swerved to miss the gate, but the cart did not. The sudden jolt upset the cart and passengers and broke one shaft and the harness connection, so the horse stumbled, continued a little farther and then turned into another yard where the gate was open.

My sisters were crying hysterically, but fortunately not physically hurt, apart from gravel rash. On the other hand, I need six stitches in the back of my head and was concussed. The good Samaritan who picked me up drove us home and then drove me to the hospital.

I thought I would be killed when I got home and truly wished to die, knowing I had endangered my sisters and feeling I had lost my horse forever. If she wasn't killed on the road, she would certainly be destined for the slaughterhouse.

Strange how the wheels of fortune turn. This was undoubtedly the worst thing I had ever done in my life, but I was reprieved. My mother must have been so relieved at having her daughters saved from near death that her anger was directed at motorbike hoons and the Sunday school, from which no one had inquired about our welfare or sent a card, when the incident had happened only a block away and everyone would know. What my stepfather thought, I never discovered, as Mum really ruled the roost where the children were concerned. Gypsy was in no danger of being slaughtered. She, in fact, became the heroine, actually choosing to go on the footpath and causing the cart to break, saving the little girls. I think Mum could understand the reason I did what I did, although I made no mention of sneaking off to look at a gymkhana.

My worst crime for her was spending the bus money on lollies.

CHAPTER 7

1955 — Family and a Helpful Counsellor

IN THE FIFTIES, FAMILY dynamics were different. Father was usually the sole breadwinner and the senior disciplinarian. 'Wait until your father gets home' was a commonly heard threat. Father was also the lord of outside the home, the lawn, the shed, the barbecue and, for those affluent enough to own one, the car. Finally, he was the general fixer of all things broken and those malfunctioning. Mother was the domestic queen of inside the house and the children. Unfortunately, in 1955, my mother was quite unwell, and as I had been second mother to her brood since the age of seven, I now had to do most of the heavy domestic chores as well. Saturday became washing day, boiling sheets and whites in the copper, rinsing in the concrete tub and then feeding items through the mangle before hanging them on the line.

I should mention here memories of my siblings at this stage. Margaret (or Peggy as she was now called), my longed-for baby sister, had been sickly from birth, regularly regurgitating food and failing to thrive. Years later, it was discovered she had been born with a faulty pancreas that caused this problem and the onset of diabetes type 1. As a toddler, she was full of life, determination and a definite streak of stubbornness. She had a very mobile face where every emotion registered, starry eyed with pleasure or heavy browed with frustration and mouth set in stubborn refusal. It seemed as if she was always there with me, going to school, to Sunday school, to piano lessons. Wherever I went, she assumed she would go too. Always ready to help with animals, she took over the baby lambs I brought home from Flemington, bottle feeding them and crying over their deaths. Eager to follow me wherever I went, she would hop up behind me on Gypsy and happily ride for miles, even after our disastrous trip in the cart. At my second visit to Fairfield Gymkhana, Margaret was entered in the under-seven rider class, and the judge was so impressed with her handling of a big horse, he gave her second prize.

Rosemary was a totally different baby; she seemed never to cry. Angelic face with big blue eyes and golden curls, she seemed to live in a world of her own. Nervous and shy, she hid away, happy to cuddle a doll and be left alone. All animals frightened her; the dog barking made her cry, the cat leaping onto her bed left her hysterical, and the horse was definitely a no-no. Rosemary was the beautiful, easily managed baby, until the baby boy arrived three years later.

Owen was the longed-for son and seemingly a beautiful, healthy baby. Big blue eyes, golden hair, chubby features in that adorable cherub way and a beautiful smile. He was very slow at achieving baby milestones, crawling, walking and speech, and seemed to have muscle weakness. In his second year, he became a demon child, throwing himself on the ground, screaming, banging his head on the wall and totally unable to control his tantrums. Before the onset, he would glow with a pink tinge on his face, hands and feet and be constantly itching.

Shut in his room, he would scream until near convulsing, with choking, heaving sobs. Smacking did not solve the problem. Finally, Mum took him to a doctor, who said that he had pink disease and that keeping him in a darkened room might help. This disease was said to be supersensitive to mercury, which was used in some medicines at this time. Later, pink disease would be linked to autism, but back in 1954, we hadn't heard of that word. Owen had already been impossible to take shopping as he frequently threw tantrums there, so now we three sisters were co-opted to mind the new toddler, playing games in a darkened room.

Back at school in 1955, I had an interview with a lady I hadn't seen before. I think she must have been a school counsellor. I hadn't realised that the school would want to check on a student who went home every sports afternoon to help her mother. This lady wanted to know all about my home circumstances, what household chores

I did, what were my siblings like, where I did my homework, and what plans I had for my future. So I told her all about my life. Mum was unwell most of the time, and as I was the oldest, I did most of the household chores, the other children being too small to be much use. I probably waxed lyrical about the problems with the baby boy, how his screaming drove us all mad. I said I shared a room with my two sisters and did my homework on the dining table after I had washed up. My ambition was to become a vet and move to the country where I could have horses. At no stage did I mention working and owning a horse.

The lady took copious notes and then told me that in NSW, there was a special holiday home, called Stewart House, that gave school students who were having a difficult time a free holiday by the sea. There were teachers there who would help with homework and doctors who would check you over. Places were generally offered to primary schoolchildren, but she thought I was a deserving case, so she would see what she could do for me. As my school, Burwood High, drew from a reasonably affluent area, she had probably not encountered a disadvantaged student before and was eager to help me. Did I think my mum could spare me for a few days' holiday by the sea? With my experience of trying to swim at Manly still vivid in my mind, I wasn't overly enthusiastic but said I would take the brochure and admission form home to my mum. She, of course, was thrilled for me and happily signed the application form.

Late summer in 1955 was very wet, with thunderstorms and driving rain. Suddenly, nobody, including my stepfather, wanted a horse in their backyard. I was now faced with the difficulties of owning a horse, who looked so miserable tethered in an open paddock in the pouring rain. Jim, the shearing shed manager, suggested I take Gypsy back to her old covered yard at Flemington, and he would feed her for me until the weather improved, so I happily agreed.

Gypsy had flourished under my care, and bossman said I had done such a good job with training her that he had another youngster I could try. This was Queen, a beautiful two-year-old roan filly, who had been mouthed and ridden once or twice. Now I had to have a saddle, and as a late Xmas early birthday present, I was given a second-hand stock saddle, one that would keep me in if Queen bucked. I didn't have the same length of time to bond with Queen; one week she arrived; the next I was on her back. Maybe because I was very gentle with her, she never tried to buck me off.

Then the astounding proposition:

Country people believe the best way to break a horse in is to put it to work, a long, steady ride droving, just walking, some trotting and occasional canter. Are you up for it?

The plan was to drive nearly to Goulburn and ride home. A trip of about two to three days. How could I get away with this?

Suddenly, I remembered the Stewart House offer. Could I tell Mum I had been offered a holiday there in the coming Easter break so as not to need an absence note?

Amazingly, the plan succeeded, and I was off to north of Goulburn to ride this two-year-old filly that I had only walked and trotted around a yard, all without a single riding lesson, just a few tips from the blokes who had watched me. To our destination of Mulgoa was a distance of about ninety miles, so riding thirty miles a day, we would do it in three days. If something went wrong, we could just load her into the float and drive home.

That part was easy; riding along the back roads was easy. What I hadn't reckoned with was camping out with a man old enough to be my grandfather and keeping his wandering hands in restraint. Just the first night, becoming increasingly worried that I was out of my depth in this situation, I dissolved into a hysterical sobbing mess, and once again I found myself in control. Gently, he held me, stroked me and calmed me down, saying he would never hurt and violate me; he only wanted to cuddle me.

These two adventures with dirty old men appeared to me to be in sharp contrast to the only other relationship I had with a man, that is, my stepfather, who, it seemed to me, took great delight in hurting me and had never cuddled me.

CHAPTER 8

1956 – In the Papers

ONCE WE WERE BACK at the shearing shed, I wanted to ride Gypsy home again as she had been kept there while I was away. The bossman revealed he wanted me to continue coming to Flemington and riding Queen, who really was a much better horse for me. I could take her to shows, and she could do well.

But I had given my heart to Gypsy. I had worked to buy her and had lavished her with love and devotion, and she had flourished under this care. I couldn't suddenly turn my affections to this new horse, even though she had been much nicer to ride and was very stylish.

Then came the bombshell. In our absence, a friend had taken Gypsy to do a trial at Harold Park. As a two-year-old, she had failed the time test, but now as a three-year-old, in her last chance at becoming a fully registered pacer, she had passed. It would mean a few races to establish a profile. Afterwards, she could be sent to stud and hopefully raise a worthwhile foal. Then I could have her back, and in the meantime, I had this beautiful mare to ride. Incidentally, I could not by law own a registered trotter until I was twenty-one, seven years away.

I was absolutely dumbstruck, lost for words to explain how I felt about trotting races in general, how they flogged the horses to the finishing line, how there was no love for the animals; they were just racing machines at the end of their career, destined to become dog food.

Sadly, I made my way home on the train, wracking my brains for a solution.

First check the facts: If she was now registered, she must have a name. I know she didn't have one last year.

Secondly, was it true that you had to be over twenty-one to own a registered horse?

At home, Mum wanted to quiz me about the holiday house and put my reticence down to tiredness. Brown from days in the sun, I was physically and mentally exhausted.

The next morning, I went to talk to my friend down the street, a grandmother of two young girls, who had once lived with her and loved having Gypsy in their yard. I thought she would know the answer to my second question as she followed racing and the trots. Her suggestion was to ring the sports announcer at 2GB who, she said, knew everything about all forms of racing. So she did, and he confirmed my fears; I was not legally able to own a registered horse, so my claims to Gypsy were worthless.

Next, was she really registered? So I put on a brave face and arrived at the shearing shed to ride Queen and say goodbye to Gypsy. There I asked what her racing name was going to be as I would like to follow her progress. The owner was so proud to say she had been registered as Gypsy Heather. He had wanted Gypsy Rose, but that name was already taken, and then he showed me her time trial, easily exceeding the minimum requirement.

I went home determined I had to do something drastic. I waited until the first Monday back at school and, with jeans in my bag, went to Flemington saleyards.

The shearing shed was closed, but I wriggled into the board through a sheep chute, removing my saddle and bridle the same way. Finally, I was off to the paddock to collect Gypsy. Then I rode to the dairy near home, waiting around until Bobby came home from school. I wanted to hide Gypsy somewhere she wouldn't be found, and he agreed to put her into the same barn where the infamous sulky had been stored. I promised to pay for the hay he gave her and would be back the following day.

My uniform looked a little worse for wear, having been stuffed in my bag all day (but I had deliberately left the hat at home), and I must have looked terrible as my mother asked if I was unwell.

The following day, I stayed in bed, feigning sickness. Mum had gone to the shops, and I was minding Owen when Jim arrived at our door. He asked me if I had taken Gypsy, and when I said no, he said,

'Well, someone broke in and stole your bridle and saddle as well as took the horse from the paddock. That horse is a valuable registered pacer, and I have reported the theft to the police. They will be interviewing you and will take the horse away. Tell me where she is and I will take her now, and I will tell the police it was a mistake'.

Strangely, I felt so strongly that this man must not have my horse, so I called his bluff and repeated, 'I did not take her. You have lost her'.

After he left, I thought over my options. I knew I did not have any legal right to the horse; the twenty pounds I had paid could probably be listed as a leasing payment for riding her. If anyone would seriously look for the horse in my district, it wouldn't take long to find her. I had to take her farther away and try and hide her in a larger paddock with other horses. The only place I knew that had such paddocks was in the Lansdowne region, where I had ridden once.

The following morning, I left early for school. In my bag were jeans, jumper, raincoat, half a loaf of bread, carrots and two apples. Under my arm was a blanket taken from my bed. The bucket and tethering rope I had taken to the dairy the previous day. I saw Bobby leaving for school and told him my plan. He said he would ride up to Lansdowne Bridge after school and bring me some food. Only problem was neither of us owned a watch. I would have to look out for school kids coming home and hang about the bridge until he came. So with school clothes left in the shed, blanket under the saddle, rope around the horse's neck and provisions in a bag in the bucket which I carried, I set out to ride to Lansdowne.

I found the paddocks fairly quickly and enquired about agistment. Suddenly, I was faced with the reality of owning a horse. Agistment cost was more than all the money I had, and payment was required for a month in advance. That option was closed. Knowing my mother would be worrying, I rode into Cabramatta, tied Gypsy up outside the Post Office and sent a telegram:

'Have taken Gypsy and gone. Don't worry. Letter following. Maureen'

Then I rode back to Lansdowne Bridge to ponder my options and wait for Bobby. Feeding myself loomed as a large problem, so I rode to the market gardens nearby and stole cobs of corn and tomatoes to supplement my rations. Riding to the main road to hopefully see children homeward bound, I filled my bucket at a front tap to give Gypsy a drink. Whether there were no children living on that stretch of road or whether my sense of timing was way out, I didn't see a single school bus or child.

Returning to Lansdowne Bridge, I unsaddled the horse, shared my corn cobs and bread, tethered her and curled up in my blanket to await the arrival of Bobby or daybreak. The night was long and cold, even though I was wearing a jumper, and the early-morning dew soaked through everything, so I was cold, tired and miserable as I tried to plan ahead.

Without a map or any idea where I could go, I thought I would just follow the areas of free grass to tether my horse and try to steal food to keep alive. So early morning, I moved from the bridge, up the hill, where the grass was more abundant and was gazing down to the road, when I saw a grey horse galloping towards the bridge. Yes, it was Bobby, having taken a day off school, with the permission of his parents, to come and find me. The only food he brought was a sandwich and an apple, but he also had last night's paper, saying excitedly,

'You are on page 3, look, a photo of you and Gypsy, and it says to come home; you can keep the horse!'

I couldn't believe my eyes. It was a lovely picture; I was standing, gazing at Gypsy with such a look of devotion, and she was nuzzling into my stomach after the treats I had in my pocket. The story said that it was all a misunderstanding, that I had thought the horse was going to the abattoir and I had run away to save her. The last part at least was true. But most important of all, it said that my mother was pleading for her daughter to return home and that she will be able to keep the horse.

I had never kissed a boy, but I felt like kissing Bobby at that moment. He had told his Mum that he thought he knew where I would head, so she agreed that he take the day off school to find me. I would be eternally grateful to her. So I packed up the gear, and together, we rode home.

I really thought I would be thrashed within an inch of my life, but once again, when I did something really bad, fortune seemed to smile on me. Mum welcomed me home with open arms. She told me that the lovely lady with racing knowledge from down the street had told her that I couldn't legally own a registered pacer and that the owner was about to race her. Mum shared my opinion of horse racing in general and could understand why I had taken the horse and run away. Then that lovely lady, with her phone, had rung the shearing shed to tell Jim that she felt the police should be investigating him and that if he took the horse, she would tell the police about his use of horses to trap underage girls. That did the trick. I heard no more from Jim, and I never went to Flemington saleyards again.

CHAPTER 9

One Good Turn Deserves Another

I GUESS I MUST have felt very lucky that I had escaped my just desserts for frightening everyone so badly, especially my mother. Probably I felt a little cocky as well, having overcome seemingly impossible odds to keep my horse. How lucky was I that the one person I turned to for help actually had a phone? Without a phone, my mother couldn't check to see whether what her daughter had told her about the trip to a holiday home was true. She would have had to walk to the main road to use the public phone booth that never had a phonebook to check the number and often was out of order, vandalised to get the coins needed for a call.

I was so grateful to the lady who followed racing that I took a saleable bag of manure down and dug it into her garden. That was when I discovered that her daughter was now living with a new fellow her mum did not like, so now the grandmother did not see her grandchildren at all. I realise that she really missed her grandchildren, and this piece of knowledge stayed with me. At school, only my best friends knew about my escapade, and I was sure none of the teachers had recognised me in the photo if they had seen it. Owning a horse did not fit into their picture of me as an underprivileged child, the eldest of four, and Villawood was a long way from Burwood.

Earning money was now a real problem, so I stepped up my efforts at selling manure, although without the cart, this was more difficult. Travelling farther afield one Saturday, I was canvassing a new street when I heard a girl call Gypsy by name. It was Janice, the older of the two grandchildren who looked to be about eight. Her sister Julie, aged about six, was there also, together with four or five other kids, playing in the street. Immediately, I told all the children that if they asked their respective parents if anyone wanted to buy a bag of horse manure for the garden, I would give them a ride on my horse. So I took each child separately, going farther down the street, leaving Janice and Julie till last. Then I said,

'Do you want to go and visit your grandmother with me? I can get you there and back before dark, and if your mum comes looking for you, these kids can say I kidnapped you, so you won't get into trouble'.

Janice was eager for an adventure, but Julie was hesitant, saying, 'I have to ask Mum'.

I told her I was kidnapping Janice, and if she wanted to see her grandmother, she could come too; otherwise, go and tell your mum.

She reluctantly agreed, and with her in front and Janice behind, I set sail for home after telling the other children I was taking these two to visit their grandmother.

It was less than a half-hour ride, and the look of astonishment and joy on their grandmother's face was enough for me to brave the charge of kidnapper if that came to pass. Their mother had to wait for her boyfriend to get home from wherever before they could pick up their children, although she did have a very heated conversation with her mother over the phone.

Some days later, I had a very stern lecture from the local policeman, who threatened me with being sent to Parramatta Girls Home now that two incidents were listed against me.

'Horse theft and kidnapping, criminals have been hanged for that. We could charge you with being uncontrollable, and you would be in a reform school until your eighteenth birthday. What would happen to your horse then?' was his final blood-curdling threat.

Fortunately, my mother once again took my part, showing my school records to prove what a diligent student I was, not just some tearaway delinquent. I remember her saying that I tended to get carried away at seeming injustices.

Also, rather fortunately, my stepfather was still at work during this visit, although incidentally, after I ran away, he never raised a hand against me again.

Nevertheless, I was determined to become a responsible law-abiding citizen after that.

CHAPTER 10

1956 — A New House and More Babies

ONE GOOD THING ABOUT having a boy in the family was we were eligible for a three-bedroom house, and soon we were to move to one in Chullora.

It is not easy to move when your household includes four children, one horse, one dog, a pair of bantams and a cat that had just given birth to five kittens. We did not have a car to assist. No one in our immediate family drove, not Mum, Dad, Nana, not even Uncle Eddie or Aunt Esther! A removalist van was hired, and Dad went with them to open up the house, taking the dog on a lead and the bantams in a chaff bag. Nan came to help Mum with the children on a bus to Granville, a train to Strathfield and a bus to Greenacre. I was left to work out a route to ride Gypsy and deal with the cat and kittens. The mother cat had disappeared at first sight of our packing to move, so I decided to leave the kittens snug and warm in a box on the back veranda in the hope their mum would return.

Once again, using a neighbour's street directory, I plotted my route via Auburn, Lidcombe, through Rookwood Cemetery, cross the Hume Highway and along to Keira Ave Chullora. Apart from becoming totally lost in the cemetery, I managed the ride in about three hours. Unfortunately, when I rode back to Villawood the following day, the mother cat had deserted her family, and the kittens were cold and stiff in the box.

At the back of the new house was a huge paddock with a derelict farmhouse, complete with barn, absolutely perfect for me. The remainder of this original property housed the Chullora Drive-In, and we could actually see the screen from our bedroom window, like watching a silent movie. I didn't have to travel far now to Burwood High, but once again, my mother caught a bus to enrol my sisters at South Strathfield Primary School when Greenacre Public School was closer.

At this stage of my life, I desperately needed a job; my savings from the shearing shed wage were nearly depleted. Bankstown was the closest biggest shopping centre, a bus ride away, and I diligently went looking for work. Woolworths said to come back when I turned fourteen and nine months (the earliest official time to legally leave school). Fortunately, a little cafe was desperately in need of a kitchen hand to wash dishes and make sandwiches and didn't require my birth certificate, so I went to work on the weekends. This not only kept Gypsy in shoes and chaff but also started the fund to buy a second horse, hopefully a jumper, as soon I was to discover a pacer is not really the most appropriate horse to own.

I joined the Pony Club at South Strathfield and met a totally different type of horse owner to the ones I had known at Villawood. The founding couple of the Pony Club had a son who was disabled, having suffered polio. He loved animals, especially horses, so they bought the adjoining property and turned it into 'Robert's Corral'. This included a yard big enough for a dozen horses, a tack room, three stables and space for a small cart. Robert did not have any strength in his legs to be able to ride, but he could handle a pony in a cart.

Other children with horses were invited to come to the corral for a sausage sizzle and games day once a month. It was here that I discovered my horse was really unsuitable, as was my stock saddle. The other riders were very competitive, going to shows and winning ribbons.

One of the girls had a beautiful pony but really needed a bigger horse as she was now sixteen and tall. Her parents said she had to get her pony eligible for the Royal Easter Show, and then they would sell it and buy a bigger horse. As I was under fifteen, I could ride it in different events for her and help her win points to earn her way to the Royal.

With all this concentration on the horses in my life, I had left out significant events that happened to my family. First of all, late in

1955, Mum was obviously pregnant again. I was absolutely furious, having believed that having finally achieved a son, my parents would be satisfied with just four children. Most of my friends came from two-child families, occasionally a third child, but no one else had four, let alone five children in their family. Inevitably, the task of a second mother would fall to me, as Margaret was only seven, and I was totally over babies; I now had a horse I wanted to pamper.

Also, Mum had not been well during her last pregnancy, and I was a little fearful that this time, it could be worse. Having had just a smattering of sex education lessons, I could not believe that people as old as my parents had sex just for fun. Once they had achieved a son, that should be it, but when I voiced this opinion, along with my fears for her safety, Mum only laughed. Imagine my horror when on 26 April 1956, my mother gave birth to twins, a boy, Ian, and a girl, Pat.

Now I was bottle feeding babies as well as trying to pacify a very difficult toddler.

Fortunately, Owen loved having a ride on Gypsy. I still had to rush off to my job at the cafe and try to fit homework into the very few quiet times at home. The moments spent riding my horse were snatches of serenity in a noisy, demanding world.

Nana had been a frequent visitor during Mum's final pregnancy and the twins' early years, but then she found a gentleman friend, Harry Jones, who took her dancing, and her visits became fewer. Her social life was expanding, and she kept in close contact with her sister Lottie and her brother Bob. We never saw these relatives, as without a car, transporting small children was a problem.

In the September holidays of 1956, now aged fourteen years and nine months, I returned to Woolworths to apply for a job. In the fifties, Woolworths was like a big 'reject' shop. They were not a supermarket then; the only food sold was on the confectionary counter. The store consisted of rows of counters of goods with a salesperson for each type of merchandise and an old-fashioned cash register for which they were also responsible. At a quarter to nine, we would start removing the dust covers from the counters, counting the money into the till and fixing the receipt roll. At the end of the day (five thirty, no late-night shopping then), we would total the receipts, count out the money and pray the two would match, as if you were short, you would have to make up the difference. This led to very careful counting of change. Then we would replace dust covers, all of which took nearly half an hour, which wasn't included in the pay packet. At that stage, junior wage was about one pound ten shillings per day and ten shillings sixpence on Saturday. At least it was a regular income to pay for feed and shoeing.

At the end of that term, having completed the Intermediate Certificate, I was contemplating applying to Tommy Smith's racing stables for the position of strapper when my school informed me that I had been awarded the Old Girls' Scholarship to complete my matriculation education. My mum was thrilled, and as I already had a full-time January job at Woolworths and continuation of Saturday work, I agreed fourth form brought new interests, captaining the debating team, competing against other schools and attending a performance of the opera *Carmen* at the Elizabethan Theatre. This last event was a special night out with my nan, and what a magnificent introduction to opera it was. Such stirring music, magnificent costumes and a feisty heroine who stirred the latent feminist within me. I vowed that would not be my last visit to the Opera, and my biggest regret was that when our magnificent Opera House opened, I could not take my nan as she had sadly passed away two years before.

That was also the year I stayed at the Easter Show, fell in love with a stuntman and bought my jumper, Rajah.

CHAPTER 11

1957 – Staying at the Easter Show

BARBARA HAD ACQUIRED ENOUGH points to be able to enter her pony, Jane, into the Sydney Royal Easter Show. The country friends of her family also had horses in the show, and I was invited to stay with Barbara at the showground to help out. This involved getting up at five thirty in the morning to muck out stables as the cleaners had to remove this refuse before the crowds arrived at nine. I would then feed and brush the horses, and if I was really lucky and the owner didn't turn up, I could exercise them. As it happened, the pony's owner, a thirteen-year-old girl, was more interested in staying in town with her mother, visiting shops and seeing movies on the days she didn't have to compete, so I could pretend this gorgeous pony was mine.

I was even able to ride it in the Grand Parade as it was obligatory for all horses who had competed that day to be in the parade, and having competed in the morning, the owner wanted to see a movie that afternoon. One of my earlier goals achieved! Actually, that was my second appearance in the parade as this country family also exhibited cattle and had asked me to lead a very gentle dairy cow in the parade. I was happy to do anything to please these people and felt so lucky just to be there, participating. They were so pleased with me that they paid me ten pounds for five days' work. A fortune for doing something I loved and would have done for free!

This was also the time of my first real boyfriend crush.

Once again, a friend of this family had come to see and advise on their new horse.

He was tall, tanned and broad shouldered, with beautiful blue eyes that crinkled in his smiling face. Just the image I had dreamed about when I pictured my unknown father. He was also probably old enough to be my father, but that didn't matter to me. Watching the way, he handled the skittish horse and how great he looked riding it, I was smitten. Later I was told that he had been Robert Mitchum's understudy in the movie *The Sundowners*. He had done all the riding and the difficult stunts.

Wow! I was talking to a real live movie star, even though his name was very low down in the credits. At some stage, I told him I really wasn't into show riding, but I wanted to buy a horse that could jump. He told me he was friends with Lionel Ware, who travelled the country, buying horses to be used in movies and television shows.

'I'll ask him to look out for one for you' was his parting remark, and I was left starry eyed, full of rapture.

Throughout those six days of the show, he took Barbara and me to dinner and on all the scary rides, which I really hated, but I had to pretend to love being scared out of my wits. Every year, until Owen arrived, my family had gone to the show, but never had I been on any fairground ride, not there or anywhere. The stuntman knew I was underage, and he treated me with care and kindness. I felt totally safe in his hands as I tried to show him that I was brave enough to ride a horse over jumps.

After the show finished, things went back to normal, until some months later, Barbara rode her new horse to my place to tell me to be at Robert's Corral the following day. Her family had been contacted by Stuntman, who told them that Lionel Ware had a horse that kept jumping out of the stable.

I couldn't sleep that night, wondering whether I was really doing the right thing. Could I possibly control a country horse that wants to be free, jumping out of his stable?

The following day, I rode Gypsy to the corral, telling her that I would always love and care for her; I would not trade her in on a new fad.

The stunt rider was there with a large ute, and we drove to Leichardt, where Lionel Ware had a huge stable complex with old-fashioned carriages lining the walls and dozens of horses gazing out over stable doors. We walked past these to a large dirt yard, where two bay horses stood together in a corner.

'He just needs company', said Lionel. 'There's not a mean bone in his body, and he would have been great for what I need, but he hates to be shut up in a stable and can't bear to be alone, even out here. He'll jump out, so he is just a pain in the neck to me. Twenty-five pounds and he's yours. He was part of a job lot I bought, so I reckon that covers his cost'.

He and Stuntman then had a conversation, and suddenly, I could have the horse for twenty pounds, exactly the amount of money I had saved.

I looked at this beautiful rich bay gelding, much bigger than Gypsy, but solidly proportioned and with such a gentle look in his eye. He checked the teeth, mature but not old, and felt the legs for splints, clean. Then bridle and saddle on, Stuntman swung aboard. Round the yard at a canter, flying change to opposite direction, burst of speed, sudden halt, rein back. Then it was my turn. Walk, trot, canter, change direction, halt, rein back, all smoothly executed with barely a touch on the reins and minimal pressure of the legs.

'Well, I think he's a good buy. He seems steady and reliable, and he will teach you how to ride over jumps'.

Final word of approval from Stuntman and I had bought myself a horse.

Lionel was happy to lend us a float that Stuntman would return that afternoon, so off we go. It was a double float, so we picked up Gypsy and continued home. I took the new horse off first and came back for Gypsy as Stuntman had unloaded her. Suddenly, *whoosh*, the new horse walked to the gate, which was taller than he was and, with a tremendous standing jump, cleared the gate and walked over to Gypsy.

'Well, you were warned that is his specialty. You will have to keep the two horses together'.

Rajah proved to be an absolute joy, so gentle my young siblings could ride on him and so happy to jump I could practise over our front fence and any fallen trees I found. He was happy to be ridden away from Gypsy, but I could not take her away from him, so often she was left at home. I scoured the school and municipal libraries for books on riding and jumping and wondered how I could really train my natural jumper when I couldn't afford lessons.

Once again, Stuntman came to the rescue. It was midwinter when he turned up at my home one weekend.

'Just checking, how you are riding over jumps?'

'Well, apart from the front fence, not much'.

'I think you should join the Sydney Hunt Club. I went with a friend last week, and your horse would love it. The fences are between two and four feet, and if your horse refuses, there is always a gate to go through'.

Suddenly, I thought he wanted to buy my horse, and I didn't want to sell. But no, just an invitation too good to miss.

'Come next week and see. I have enough room for you in the truck, but we leave at six in the morning, and you have to wear a crash helmet'.

So that was how I rode with the Sydney Hunt Club at properties in Campbelltown, Leppington and Picton. The trail was set by a rider dragging a pungently smelling chaff bag over a pre-arranged route while the riders saddled up. Then the master set out, the hounds were released, the red-coated whips rode at the sides, and the rest of us followed at a respectable distance. The jumps were mainly wooden gates or rails, which could be opened by those who didn't jump, and there were several fallen trees and streams to cross.

At about eight o'clock when we started, the frost was still on the ground, the horses were frisky and raring to go, and Rajah was no exception. Stuntman's friend turned out to be a stunningly attractive blonde riding a magnificent thoroughbred with ease and skill. For a moment when we saddled up, I felt like the poor relation, with my woolly coated beast and my shabby stock saddle. However, once we were up and galloping, I would not have changed places with the queen of England as my horse charged towards the fences, ears pricked, and then sailed over. Riding over jumps was a breeze with this horse; he just loved being with others and jumped anything in the way. I was also cheered by the friendliness of the group. Several people came to welcome me and comment on my good horse. I must have been grinning from ear to ear. Another childhood dream achieved in a totally unexpected manner.

That winter with the Sydney Hunt Club led to other opportunities.

A member living in Homebush offered me to use her training paddock, complete with jumps, and by summer, Rajah and I were competing in junior showjumping events.

He was never quite as happy with this, wanting to look first and sometimes doing his famous standing jump, which was very unseating.

Still, without any formal coaching, I devoured books like *Equitation* and *Dressage* and taught myself.

The climax of that year was to compete in the one-day event held at Wilberforce, where, after a reasonable dressage test, we were eliminated at the cross-country when, instead of jumping into the water, Rajah did an enormous leap across, landing outside the flags and thus being eliminated.

The following year, having spent twelve months practising jumping into water, even going so far as to ride to Brighton and challenge the ocean, we finally finished second. Then when I was wrapped up in uni studies, I leased him to a friend who competed in that same event and won.

CHAPTER 12

January 1959 — Dunlop's Rubber Factory

JANUARY 1959: I PASSED the Leaving Certificate with four As and two Bs and had a choice of two scholarships to Sydney University. Hoping to do veterinary science, I had taken biology, chemistry, physics and mathematics and applied for a Commonwealth Scholarship. However, competition for placement in that field was keen, and I did not reach the required mark to enter. As a Commonwealth Scholarship only paid for fees, I preferred my second option, an Education Department Scholarship, also to Sydney University, but with a living-away-from-home allowance. This was quite strange, and I wondered whether, having nominated New England as my university of choice, the 'powers that be' had thought I was a country student. In reality, I really wanted to go to the country with my horses. Maybe my career advisor, who knew my family history, that I was the eldest of six with great demands on my time, had put in a special request. Whatever the reason, that mention of regular income sealed the choice, especially as at this point in time, I was again strapped for cash.

Woolworths, who had been my steady employer since I turned fourteen and nine months, terminated my services after the Christmas rush ended. At seventeen, I was officially too old. All the other places I tried already had their staff, and for two weeks, I was out of work, while the horses kept on eating.

In desperation, I found an advertisement in the local paper:

'Dunlop's Rubber Factory, needing more staff, training provided'.

Any fool can do a factory job, right? Wrong. At first, management didn't want to hire me; I wasn't the right type. When I pleaded that I had just lost my job for being too old and couldn't find another one, they relented and agreed to a two-week trial. That was the hardest two weeks of my life so far.

Situated not far from Bankstown, the factory was a large corrugated fibro shed with high unopenable windows to let in light.

Rows and rows of long trestle tables filled the room, each table having eight seated girls on either side. Down the centre was a moving runway on which travelled rubber boots in various stages of manufacture.

The group that I joined worked on slapping a pre-cut sole onto a steel anvil, shaped like an upside-down boot. Our job was to pick up the sole, slap it on the anvil and push down the sides to stick. Sounds easy, but not at the rate these girls worked. I sensed their disappointment as I was led to the table and introduced as

'Maureen, the new girl, show her what to do'.

The leader of the group really didn't have enough English to explain but pantomimed picking something up and slapping it onto the stationary anvil and smoothing the sides. Then the machinery roared into life, and in a moment, a steady stream of soft black shapes was heading our way.

The anvils were moving at a slightly slower pace, but even so, if you didn't get the sole on straight the first time, you had to chase the anvil to fix it or, most times, just let it go. Sometimes someone down the line rectified it, usually with a glare at me; sometimes the wonky sole just kept travelling.

There was no chit-chat, only the slap, slap, slap of rubber hitting steel.

This was January, and the heat in that shed was unbelievable. Sweat ran into my eyes, but I could not pause to wipe them; my hands were constantly pick, slap, smooth, and a strangled gasp as another went wrong. Two hours flat out and fifteen minutes for smoko, going to the toilet, washing your face and drinking water. Back for another two hours flat out and then forty-five minutes for lunch. That routine was repeated in the afternoon, finishing with half an hour clean-up and then home. We started at seven. No one was late, and no one left while the machinery was running. Smoko was true to the name; the majority of the workers went straight outside to smoke or at least to get fresh air as the smell of warm rubber permeated everything, including clothes and hair. I realised why the manager had said I wasn't the right type; 90 percent of the girls would have been migrant women with very little English. I doubt if many Australian girls would have lasted there.

My first lunchtime I looked for an English speaker to have a conversation as none of the girls at my table seemed to understand English. When I did find a girl to chat to, she said, 'If you think today is hard, love, wait until Friday. This is the first time your lot has had a newbie, and they don't realise what is in store. My advice to you is go home now and don't come back. This job isn't for soft kids like you'.

Probably that advice annoyed me, but I really needed the money; scholarship funds were weeks away, so I kept going.

By Friday, I had learnt how to almost keep pace, and fewer misplaced soles were getting away. The foreman came around just after the machinery had ceased and gave each of us a brown envelope. Mine contained the six pounds promised as my training wage, but every other woman on the table cried out with anger. Each person was paid piecemeal by the completed anvils on the table, and I had lowered the average for everyone. Fortunately, most of the ranting was in a language I didn't understand, but now I realised the significance of the chat I had had earlier, and I was filled with anger against the company.

How dare they treat people like this? Why didn't they train beginners together on a separate table where their average would be equivalent to their training pay?

The following week, I thought things might get better, but in fact, they were worse. That week, the temperature soared into the high thirties. The heat was unbearable, the rubber slippery to touch. Sweat blinded my eyes as I staggered on, mouth dry, throat parched with gasping, continuing to grab, slap, smooth. Grab, slap, smooth. Suddenly, an Australian man rushed in and swung a mallet at the fibro walls, making a huge window, although there wasn't a breath of air. Then he yelled, 'Stop work. Everybody out'.

Well, of course, we didn't stop until the machinery did. Then we wandered outside, ready to have another smoke. I never did discover who it was that called the strike and smashed holes in the wall, but after about thirty minutes, where we could hear male voices arguing, we went back inside, and there were other men bringing buckets of water with cups so we could drink. I think that counted as our smoko that day, but the following day, once again, we were served water in the afternoon. Then Friday arrived, and again the consternation when the wages were revealed. This time, I wasn't entirely to blame. The strike had taken the best part of an hour and the slowing for a drink had definitely set the quota back, but what a way to live your life!

When someone today says, 'Migrants will steal our jobs', I think back and say,

'No, they do the jobs Australians don't want to do often in conditions Australians wouldn't tolerate'.

CHAPTER 13

February 1959 — Off to University

FOLLOWING ACCEPTANCE OF THE teaching scholarship to Sydney University, I had to make plans for a new life in Crown St, Woolloomooloo, sharing my nana's bedsit. First was the problem of the horses. Gypsy, my ex-pacer mare, was only eight years old, with a prospective life of thirty. Here fortune smiled as a good friend from Pony Club days had won the heart of an Akubra boy at the Easter Show. Joan was about to be married and move to his country property in Merriwa.

'She can retire with us, and if a visitor needs a horse to ride around the property, she'll do'.

Gypsy became a valuable asset. Joan had acquired a sulky, and after giving birth to twin girls, she would drive the now mature and stable Gypsy around in the sulky, with the babies aboard, until they went to sleep. Later, when the family had increased to four children, Gypsy and the sulky would transport the goods needed for a camping holiday at the nearby river. Finally, aged thirty-one, Gypsy quietly went to sleep one night on that same property.

I just hated the thought of parting with Rajah. There was so much more I wanted to achieve with him, but a university scholarship was an opportunity too good to miss. Another girl at the Pony Club was as anxious to find a horse to ride over jumps as I had been, so I decided to lease Rajah to her for as long as my university studies would take. That was on the condition she kept him with the lady who had let me train in her paddock as she had other horses he could live with and not be lonely. Also, I hoped to be able to come back and ride him in the Christmas vacation. Wendy was happy with this arrangement, and the following October, riding Rajah, she won the Junior One Day Event at Wilberforce.

The living-away-from-home allowance really was just a pittance; sometimes I walked home from university as I had spent the bus fare on a coffee. So very soon I went searching for employment and was hired by David Jones to work in the packing department on Saturday mornings. The ladies in that department were lovely motherly souls who pampered me, getting me to try on fabulous fur stoles and coats before we wrapped them up and sent them on. What a change from slaving at Dunlop's!

Orientation week at Sydney University was a real eye-opener for me. The main sandstone building looked as if it had been plucked from England and deposited behind a typically English manicured lawn. As I wandered through the quadrangle, the passing professors wore traditional gowns and carried stacks of folders.

At the entrance to the old Fisher Library were two stone lions reported to roar if ever a virgin walked past. Obviously, a myth, as I sailed through. Down the street between the two cafe facilities, the Union and Manning, were dozens of stalls touting many different associations to join, concerts to attend and sporting facilities to use. Enthusiastically, I collected pamphlets, signed up for play reading and the feminist group and joined the judo club.

Play reading was somewhat daunting with so many theatrically inclined students; the feminist meetings tended to be loud, raucous and threatening; but the judo group was great. At first, we learned how to fall, which I was pretty good at from my horse-riding days. Then what a thrill to be able to toss a six-foot male onto his back.

When I finally joined the huge arts group in the main theatre and chose my four subjects, English, history, psychology and philosophy, I could not believe the amount of free time between classes and tutorials. Maybe I could have fitted in the occasional horse ride, but fortunately, I decided no. This would be the year I would let my passion slumber as I realised on a scholarship, the first failure meant out, and I planned to become a teacher, move to the country and take my horses with me.

So this was a new life for me. Gone were the jeans and boots. I now wore full skirts with rope petticoats and staggered in stiletto heels. Dance was my new leisure passion. My nana was a great mentor, teaching me waltz, foxtrot and even the Pride of Erin. Then it was off to Newtown Dance Studio to learn jive and all the Latin dances, followed by Saturday night at Surreyville Dance Hall, with the wonderful floating floor to practise. Boys were on the radar, only if they could dance, but I think I was still carrying a flame for my stuntman, and I didn't meet any boys who spoke my horse language.

At the end of the first semester, I was travelling well in my studies and had a great longing to see my horse, so I took a weekend off to go and have a ride. Back at Deidre's, the young girl was riding well over jumps and thought she might be ready to take a turn with the Sydney Hunt Club. Deidre had a new horse, a country-bred ex polo pony who could jump, and she asked if I would like to try him out. He seemed very obliging, happy to jump and easy to control. Deidre was suffering from a strained shoulder and couldn't ride, so she offered,

'How about I take both horses to the Hunt, and you can ride Dal and view your horse from a different angle'.

The following weekend saw us set off for Leppington, arriving about 8:00 a.m. When I mounted Dal, I found a very different horse to the one I had ridden the previous week. Whether it was the travelling in the float, the sight of dozens of other horses or the crisp wintry air, he was walking on tiptoes curled up, ready to spring out of his skin.

'He'll be all right once you get going', said Deidre. 'He's just a bit excited at the new environment'.

Carefully, I steered him towards the back of the group. No time to watch my horse, I was too busy dealing with the one I was on. Suddenly, the hounds were running, and we were off. Dal gave a huge leap and started galloping in earnest. The first fence caught him by surprise, and he eased his dash. Then we were galloping up a hill, and it was taking its toll on him. At the next fence, a number of horses were in front of us, so I had to swing him around to use some time before we charged at it. At last, I was starting to feel in control and enjoy the ride. Bust just as soon as you relax, something happens.

When we breasted the hill, there was a clear view in front, open pasture bisected by a wire fence, with wooden rails directly ahead.

At the bottom of the incline, the hounds and the redcoats had made a right-hand turn and were cantering away from us, towards the next patch of scrub. In an instant, Dal had snatched the reins from me and was tearing off at an angle, heading to cut the red-coated riders off before they hit the scrub. I quickly shortened the reins and tried hauling to the side to turn him from his purpose. The wire fence loomed large, no wooden capping; would he see it? Fortunately, yes, and we were sailing over. Just in time, I had given him his head to jump. Now I had to fight to get control as the gap between us and the redcoats narrowed. Next thing I knew, *thump*! Dal had sideswiped a huge grey gelding, and the redcoat, Ken Sonter, a man of at least fifteen stone, had been thrown off his horse. I had also come off in the impact, and another redcoat had just missed treading on me.

The entire hunt came to a standstill. An annoyed master rode up and said to me,

'Can you walk?' and I thought, 'Oh my god, I will have to walk home leading the horse', who was now standing like a perfect angel, having done what his polo experience had taught him to do, and that was catch and stop the opposing team.

The redcoat who had nearly run over me, jumped off his horse and said,

'Are you okay? I nearly ran you over. Look, this is a very gentle mare. You can ride her if you like. I'll take the new fellow and teach him some hunt manners'.

So I moved to the back of the field and very sedately finished the ride. When I collected Dal, his rider said,

'This fellow can certainly jump, but I think he needs a man to ride him. I'll spread the word around'.

He and Deidre had a long conversation, and Deidre said later,

'Thank goodness no one was injured, but that actually has been the best thing that could have happened to me. I should get a good price for the horse'.

As for me, that was my last ride with the Sydney Hunt Club. I went back to my studies and, come summer holidays, decided to do showjumping instead.

CHAPTER 14

1960 – I Meet a Quiz Champion

IN JANUARY 1960, HAVING passed my exams, I was living back at home and going out with a would-be boyfriend, Alan, who told me he knew someone I should meet. His brother Dave had met this chap while in the North Coast and had brought him to Sydney to try his luck in quiz shows.

'He is such a smart guy, knows everything and would love to meet a university student like you'. I was really quite tired of young university men who knew everything and couldn't resist letting everyone know how smart they were.

'No, this guy is different. He is older and a war hero. He even has a VC'.

Now that sparked my interest, and I agreed to go out to dinner with both of them.

The man was much older than I, quite good looking in the rugged outdoor sense I liked, so I flirted a little. After all, Alan wanted me to make a good impression. Then if he were upset at my behaviour, it was his fault. Over dinner, I asked about his war experiences, but he didn't want to talk about that. He asked me what subjects I was studying and then asked me the most obscure questions about historical incidents. When I didn't know, he replied in such detail I was amazed and thought, 'Wow, what a history buff'.

Then he switched to English literature, and although I fared better there, he was still definitely more knowledgeable.

'Wait till he starts on science', said Alan. 'He is a walking encyclopaedia. He has applied to go on a quiz show and should win a heap of money'.

He replied that he had left school at thirteen to work on his father's dairy farm but had educated himself by reading the Encyclopaedia

Britannica by the light of a kerosene lamp. I was so impressed, I continued to play the quiz game and marvelled at his incredible memory. He then asked me to go out to dinner with him without Alan, and in the spirit of investigating a strange creature, I agreed.

This time, he was more interested in asking me questions about myself. He liked my Irish-sounding name, as his dad, Patrick, was called Paddy; that I was English, so was his mum; that I came from a large family, as he was one of five; and that we were born in the same month, November, although I was the deep, dark, deadly Scorpio and he was the more easygoing Sagittarius. I told him I was training to become a teacher and wanted to go to the country to work.

Apparently, I ticked all the right boxes for him because in the space of that one dinner date, he went from testing my knowledge to considering me as a life partner. He told me that he was expecting to win a large amount of money doing quiz shows and would build a new house on his dad's property and that he had a reasonable income from his service pension and was paid to do trips to Canberra and appear as our only living VC recipient. He didn't like living in the city but had found country girls were not very intelligent. Also, he confided that he really didn't know how to talk to girls and do the romantic stuff. Suddenly, February and a return to university life couldn't come fast enough. Later that week, I rang Alan to tell him I couldn't play quiz games with his mate anymore as I was moving back to town to prepare for a difficult year. That man went on to be a star on a quiz show and shortly after married a nurse from Turramurra. I was not invited to the wedding.

CHAPTER 15

1960 – I Become a Night Nurse

AT THE START OF the second year at university, I really felt too grown up to be living with my grandmother. I decided to use my living-away-from-home allowance to share accommodation with a classmate. Fran hailed from Dubbo, was doing the same course as I was and, as a country student, had been boarding at a hostel. We both thought sharing a room would be a good move. She found a house near the station at Summer Hill, four bedrooms shared by seven girls, with a large kitchen, lounge and bathroom. The other girls were friendly, and everything seemed to work well.

One of the girls was a registered nurse who worked at a nursing home in the same street. She spoke to me one morning as we made breakfast.

'You don't seem to be wrapped up in a boyfriend. Would you like to earn money on a Saturday night? The boss keeps employing young girls to work night shift, and invariably on Saturday night, they let us down, and I finish up working a double shift'.

'I don't have any training. What if someone was really ill?'

'You don't have to have any training. It is just common sense. You walk around checking that they are okay, and there are a couple of bedridden cases you have to wash. If anything happens, the matron sleeps out back, so you just go and wake her'.

So I visited the nursing home, and the matron showed me around. I did an unpaid shift with Kathy, my housemate, who showed me how to change a bed with a patient still in it, wash a crippled man and treat his bed sores. Then I had my first shift alone, starting at 9pm checking everyone and then washing a lady. Men were upstairs, ladies downstairs, a long flight of stairs connecting the two. No buzzers or bells, patients would just call 'nurse'! Sometimes I had to run upstairs if a particularly loud-mouthed male was shouting, fearing he would wake everyone and I wouldn't be able to cope. But I had the feeling most patients had a sleeping pill to keep them calm until daybreak. That was when chaos occurred. I learned to get the washing done early and found the patients fairly comatose at that time.

My first death was a real learning experience. The lady had been expected to die for some weeks. She was just hanging on, in great pain and under heavy medication. Her daughter had tried to stay with her but had left in utter exhaustion. When I arrived that fateful night, the matron said,

'I think she will go tonight, so I am going to stay up and do paperwork. I will check her hourly'.

In the early hours of the morning, the lady did pass away. She had already been moved to a tiny room, just big enough for one bed, and the matron asked me to come and help lay her out. I had never seen a dead person up close before and was struck by how unlifelike she looked. The matron instructed me in stuffing all the bodily cavities, even up her nose and in her mouth. When we were finished, I marvelled at how peaceful she looked, not like the pain-filled face of yesterday or even the unreal face of an hour before. With brushed hair, a new nightgown and just the faintest touch of perfume, she was ready for her daughter to say goodbye. I had learned so much about life and death in that one evening.

I enjoyed my time working at the nursing home but was also determined never to be admitted to one if I could avoid it. My co-worker housemate told me a story about a nurse she had known who was having marital troubles and tried to pull her husband into line by pretending to commit suicide. This involved drinking a large quantity of scotch and taking a large dose of sleeping pills. She had done it once before successfully, not enough of both to actually kill her, just a trip to the hospital. However, the second time, either she miscalculated or she really did want to end it, and that was the tragic result.

I resolved to remember this combination if ever a nursing home seemed a probability for me.

Come spring, the horse show season had started, and Wendy, the young girl who had leased Rajah, was about to compete in the showjumping at Granville showground. Granville was a small showground and didn't require a performance record to compete as big names didn't bother going there. I asked Wendy if she minded if I came too as I would be in a different age group to her.

Unfortunately, the novice showjumping was on Saturday, but I reasoned I didn't start work until 9 pm, plenty of time to get home, shower and get to work.

Saturday dawned bright and clear, and we were in good time at the showground to practise over the warm-up jumps. Junior riders went first, and although Rajah had jumped the practise jumps with no trouble, he baulked at the real thing. Three refusals and that was it. Poor Wendy was so upset, she didn't know what she had done wrong.

'Don't worry', said Deidre, 'sometimes good horses have bad days. Go and jump him over the practise jump again so he doesn't finish on a refusal'.

So she rode him at the jump, and he sailed over effortlessly.

Then it was my turn. Once again, no problem with the practise jump, but as I rode into the ring, I could feel a sudden tension in him. I cantered two tight circles to get his attention and then rode firmly at the first jump. No problem, he flew over. Second jump and the third he cleared with ease, so I began to relax.

Bad move. The next jump was a double over the first and then a baulk at the second part. 'Drat, I'll have to jump both again', I thought as I started to turn him, but he had other ideas. He had never jumped a double before. Now, having inspected the second fence, he then decided to do a standing leap over it. As I was not facing forward, I was thrown off. This upset his jump, and he knocked the pole down and fell as well. I can vividly remember the sight of the horse over me as I hit the ground, and then the ambos were rushing to pick me up and stretcher me off the field.

I was more embarrassed than injured and quickly told everyone I was fine, except for a torn shirt. The medics insisted on checking everything and then agreed that I seemed to be okay but warned me to be careful: 'If you feel dizzy or nauseous, go to hospital'.

Rajah was unhurt from his fall, so we packed up and went home.

My boyfriend Alan, whom I had persuaded to drive me to the show, wanted to take me to a hospital there and then, but I convinced him I just needed to go home and rest. I hadn't actually told him about going to work, so I was able to bid him a fond farewell about 5pm and have a little lie-down before getting ready. I didn't feel like dinner but reasoned I'd had a hamburger for lunch, so just a cup of tea, shower and off to work.

Matron asked if I were feeling okay, and I replied I was fine, just a little tired.

I really can't remember what I achieved that night, whether I washed any patients or answered any calls. All I remember is opening my eyes to broad daylight and finding myself in bed in the downstairs ladies' ward with all the patients staring at me.

The matron had been awakened by male patients shouting and had found me unconscious on the floor. The emergency doctor was called and had helped the matron put me into bed and advised that I go to hospital the following day.

The hospital diagnosed concussion and chipped cheek bone. Needless to say, I lost my job at the nursing home.

CHAPTER 16

January 1961 – Sydney Teachers' College

CHRISTMAS HOLIDAYS 1960, I was back at home. Alan, my would-be boyfriend, was very solicitous at this time. Since I had refused any more contact with his friend Frank, he had been more attentive to me, taking me on a trip to the Blue Mountains with all of my siblings, riding in the back of his ute. That's how all country kids travelled in those days before seatbelts. Another time, we drove to the Northern Beaches, where Alan started to teach me to drive his MG in the car park at Palm Beach. What a pity I didn't continue my driving lessons with Alan; my life could have taken a different turn.

During the October long weekend, we went to the snowfields, although there wasn't much snow. We did walk the track towards to Mt Kosciusko and met two beautiful dogs. Alan was such a gentleman; I survived this trip, virgo intacta. Unfortunately, there just wasn't that passionate spark between us; we were really just very good friends.

Another thing Alan did for me was to get me a job at a nursing home in Strathfield. His parents had known the owners for years, so they were happy to do a favour for their son and give me a trial, followed by a permanent weekend night shift.

In January, I discovered I had failed one subject, English. I distinctly remembered realising, as I left the exam room, that I had totally misread a question and would no doubt fail that section. As a result of my failure, I could no longer finish my degree. I was moved into a one-year teachers' college course to enable me to teach English and history to high school students. This proved to be financially advantageous for the Department of Education as, although I had completed two thirds of a degree, I was paid as a two-year trained teacher until I finally finished the degree at my own expense.

I had a falling out with my Summer Hill flat mate, who was now engaged, anxious to become a domestic goddess and so became really upset when I didn't make it home in time for the dinner she had cooked. She had also failed her exams and was transferring to primary school teaching. As I already had the nursing job at Strathfield, I found lodging there also, sharing a room with a country girl who was attending a business studies course in town. Her parents were so relieved she would be sharing with a prospective teacher and therefore respectable. Little did they know what we did at night.

My flat mate was very happy to go dancing with me every Friday night, Vics at Strathfield, Petersham Town Hall, the Trocadero and Surreyville. The rule was one of us had to pick up a guy on his own to drive both of us home, and then we would get out of the car together, never leaving one of us alone. If the guy was really keen, he could call at our place, but we always used different names, so if he came calling, other girls at the boarding house would say, 'There is no one here by that name'. This system worked well until the day I met my future husband.

I found teachers' college far easier than university and spent most of the time there learning to play cards. One memorable occasion, I was to watch a young black African taking a class of prospective PE teachers in a dance lesson. I was mesmerised just watching him walk across the floor. He moved like oozing liquid. I would have loved to change courses but had to make do with just watching from a distance. Another pledge made deep in my soul: One day, I would dance with an African, maybe even go to Africa.

After my disastrous day at the Hunt, where my polo-trained mount Dal had charged across country to cut the leaders off and cannoned into a redcoat, throwing him from his horse, and my even more disastrous day showjumping, where my look-before-you-leap horse Rajah had thrown me off and then fallen, I had decided to leave Rajah in Wendy's capable hands and wait for a country posting to get my next horse, possibly an Arab, to do endurance riding. In the meantime, I would enjoy city life.

CHAPTER 17

1962 – The Year My Life Changed

THAT YEAR, I DID not return home for Xmas holidays but kept sharing the room with the country girl who had finished her course and now had a job. We were thinking of renting a real flat as soon as I was earning a decent teachers' wage. One fateful night in January, we went to a concert at the stadium in Rushcutters Bay and afterwards walked through Kings Cross, the notorious nightspot of Sydney. Feeling so free and worldly, we strolled down William St on route to Town Hall station. By the time we reached Crown St, we were very weary, and as we crossed the road, there was a vacant taxi, stopped at the red light. On the spur of the moment, a decision was made, and we hopped in the back seat, saying,

'Just down to Town Hall station. Thanks, driver'.

I can still remember the intense, appreciative look from the brown eyes in the rear-view mirror and the deep throaty voice as the driver asked us where we were heading and then made a strong plea to take us all the way home for a very good price. Undeterred, we waved farewell and headed down into the station. Imagine our horror when we discovered there were no trains from Town Hall until 5am and we would have to walk to Central!

Once you pass the actual Town Hall and the Trocadero, the rest of the walk to Central is pretty dispiriting, until the arches of Eddy Avenue loom into view.

Just as we were crossing the road, a taxi swirled in front of us, our original driver shouting, 'Two ladies for Strathfield, thank goodness. That fellow over there wants to go to Bondi, and I want to go west and finish for the night. Hop in, girls, and save me'.

So we did, but along Parramatta Road was an all-night takeaway coffee place where our driver just had to stop as he hadn't had dinner, and wouldn't we like a coffee too? By the time we finished coffee, cigarettes and talk, the first glimpses of dawn were showing, and I realised I had to feed my horse at Homebush. My lease arrangement was only for eleven months of the year. So tentatively, I suggested I needed to do this, and the driver, whose name I now knew was Reg, said, 'No problem', and then to my friend, 'Do you want me to drop you off home first?'

She had been well-trained and immediately said, 'Oh no, I would love to see the horse'.

So we went to Homebush, and I'm sure Rajah was amazed to see me so early but happily ate the hay I gave him.

Back to Strathfield and now the problem of not being separated. In the space of a couple of hours, I had the primal urge that I had never felt with Alan or any other boyfriend. I really wanted to kiss this man, just a good luck, happy New Year kiss, which was what he had asked for. As Carol wouldn't leave me, he kissed her and then me, but there was a lingering sensation in my kiss; we both wanted more.

That should have been it, but three nights later, he turned up about five, walked in the back door and found me in the kitchen.

'Want to come for a drive and finish our conversation? I will even have dinner if you will have it with me'.

That was the start of my mad career as a cab jockey, soliciting fares going in the right direction, Reg being able to refuse others because his fare was going a different way. All of which was totally illegal, but that didn't matter to me; I was totally caught up in the excitement of the evening. I saw places I had only heard about, Bondi, Rose Bay, Paddington, the airport, and then we had dinner at Anna's, a lovely European restaurant in Darlinghurst.

Later that evening, we parked overlooking the lights of the city and just talked for what seemed to be hours, discussing life and politics and solving world problems. I was so stimulated by the conversation, not wishing it to end. Then came the bombshell:

'I want to be straight with you and tell you I am a married man, not only a wife, but three little girls as well. There really isn't anything there any more with my wife. I can't even have a decent conversation with her, not like this with you, and I really need this mental stimulation. I won't ask anything of you, just company and conversation, but I would like to see you again. It's up to you'.

I was lost for words. I could feel the sexual attraction between us. How could he say he only wanted conversation? Why had he told me he was married? He was a good deal older than I, so I could have guessed he might be, but now it was out there in the open, and I knew I should walk away right now, but because I had been enjoying myself, I didn't want to. My head in a whirl, I just said I would think it over. When we arrived back at my home, I just waved goodbye and left.

This was probably the biggest moral question I had faced in my life so far. I knew it was morally wrong to see this man again. I had been a regular churchgoer and a Girls' Brigade leader and very recently had been saved again by attending the Billy Graham meeting and putting myself forward, needing to be reborn. This had been in the pursuit of investigating a strange phenomenon to have the emotional experience converts usually exhibit. The following day, I was back to being my agnostic self with an ever-enquiring mind.

Now as I wrestled with this new dilemma, I think I argued my way towards what I was doing was possibly a good thing. I would in no way endanger the marriage; sex was quite out of the question. If I gave him the mental stimulation he needed only as part of his working routine, then I would keep him away from other more unscrupulous females who may really end his marriage.

Thus, when he next appeared at my door, I agreed to go jockeying on the strict understanding ours was to be a mental and not a physical relationship as I would never endanger the happiness of his wife and children.

How naive and sanctimonious could a young virgin be. In truth, I just loved the exciting illegal world he had shown me, the lively banter we shared, the rapt attention he gave to my beliefs on world affairs and politics and the obvious admiration in his eyes when he looked at me. He was true to his word; apart from a friendship kiss at parting, we did not have a physical relationship, and the only weekend time we shared was the Saturday we went on a Ban the Bomb march, in which his wife would not involve his children.

In hindsight, having now experienced having another woman in a marriage, I can appreciate the facts. Firstly, the wife always suspects her husband is enamoured elsewhere. Even if there are still physical relations in the marriage, his dissatisfaction with her and his need to be elsewhere is always evident. Secondly, maybe she too ponders moving on now that the dream of happily ever after has been shattered. Reg told me his wife had made him leave once before when he was having an affair. Their subsequent reunion had led to the birth of the third child, another girl, when he had really hoped for a son. She would never take him back again.

Surely, that should have rung alarm bells in me, but no, I was too busy enjoying my very busy, very exciting life. I still worked nights at the nursing home in Strathfield, had my wonderful horse to ride and went dancing with the well-trained roommate. However, having a taxi driver did prove to be useful as when the letter came late in January that I had been posted to Rooty Hill High School, I asked him to take me there to check it out.

CHAPTER 18

1962 – My First Teaching Post

HAVING NEARLY COMPLETED AN arts degree and a one-year teaching diploma, in late January, I received my initial appointment as an English and history teacher at a new high school west of Parramatta. I hadn't heard of the place, and because I had requested a country posting, I assumed it was somewhere in the Never. Unfortunately, it was in the never-never visited territory, west of Blacktown. As I was still a learner driver, my then boyfriend, later husband, drove me there five days before the start of the school term. We found a construction site, complete with Portaloos, and a two-storey building minus a roof!

'Don't worry, love', said the cheery foreman, 'you will be boarded at Blacktown High, as we won't be finished until the Easter break. Give them a ring if you are worried'.

So I did, and a 'So sorry, no one can take your call' harassed receptionist said, 'If there is a change of venue, you will get a telegram. Otherwise, go to your appointed school'.

So I did. By 9am, seventeen bewildered staff had gathered on site. Now at least the building had a roof, but men were still working on the second level. There was a toilet block marked M and F and a temporary canteen building, and we were able to inspect the ground floor, which housed two offices, a staffroom, a sick bay and four classrooms.

Because of the noise factor, we adjourned to the extensive playground and had our staff meeting sitting on the grass under the trees. The heat was so intense, it parched the throat and dried out the nose. There was a significant majority of senior male staff members and an oversupply of young female English teachers. Thus, the English staff were given new roles: The girl who could play the piano became the music teacher, the girl who played competition basketball became the female PE teacher, and I was chosen to be future librarian. One of the manual arts men played soccer, so he became the male PE teacher.

Fortunately, we were expecting only 160 first-year students the following day, who were as new to high school as some of us were to teaching. In those days, forty students per class was the norm, so our students would fit into the four classrooms available.

It had been the boss's call to not ask to be relocated. He reasoned it was going to be an adventure for our new students; we would really be able to bond with them as we will be sharing the same difficulties. Here, we wouldn't have to deal with the problems of older, more disaffected students and the problem that our students would risk being lost in a bigger community.

Looking back, I am sure he was right. We had many days where we took kids into the playground to avoid disrupting noise, although we had been assured all major construction works in our building had been completed. Some days became impromptu sports days when staff absenteeism meant a ratio of sixty kids per staff member. There was no provision for relief staff in those days. We had music fests when the music instruments arrived, reading mornings when the library books arrived and a grand disco when the hall was built.

In 1963, when the PE teacher was largely pregnant, I became coach of the netball team and took them to Lidcombe on Saturdays to play against other teams.

In 1992, I went back for the thirty-year reunion and saw the kids who had become adults and heard their stories. I remembered them, and they remembered me, and we all agreed that those early years at high school had been a magnificent adventure. The gaining of each little benefit had been so exciting and had helped make them what they had become today. Actually, some bemoaned the fact that their kids today had things too easy.

For the first two weeks at school, I received no money at all. Scholarship money had ended the previous year, and my night nursing had paid the rent over the holiday period as my horse was still leased. Until the first pay cheque arrived, I could not give up this second job, although I was very busy preparing lessons and catching the train at 7.15am to be there at 8.30 to have much time to spend with Reg.

However, one important occasion figured largely in my growth of self-awareness.

CHAPTER 19

1962 — Ban the Bomb March

OH, THE JOY OF being nearly twenty-one, endowed with strong opinions, absolutely certain you have right on your side, and probably God too, and filled with a burning zeal to save the world from nuclear destruction. That was me on my first Ban the Bomb march through the streets of Sydney to the gathering of the chosen at the stadium in Rushcutters Bay.

I had studied two years of university modern history and knew for a fact that USA didn't need to drop the bomb on Hiroshima; they had already defeated Japan at Okinawa. Having tested their atomic and plutonium weapons on the Japanese, they were now stockpiling bombs in a deadly race with USSR. Who would be the first megalomaniac to press the button?

Surrounded by other likeminded folk, holding our CND banners aloft, waving at the police who lined the route, we felt invincible. Looking back down William St, it seemed as if the entire population of the city had joined us, waving banners stretched for miles, and the chant rang out,

> One, two, three, four
> What do you think we are fighting for?
> Five, six, seven, eight
> Peace on Earth, don't detonate,
> Ban the bomb!

Just at the entrance to the stadium, I thought a face seemed familiar. My chest tightened, my throat dried, and the chant died on my lips when I realised this man was the deputy principal at the school where I had just started as an English and history teacher. Our eyes met, and there was that fleeting moment when I felt, or rather hoped, he had not noticed me, but then the smile of recognition and a wink of conspiracy that 'I won't tell if you won't' and I could breathe again.

Inside the stadium, listening to the impassioned speakers, I felt a little bit flattened. The burning zeal had ebbed away as I realised what a fraud I was, enthusiastically supporting a cause when surrounded by sympathisers, but at the mere thought of a threat to my job, my position in society, I wanted to run and hide.

Back at school on Monday, I endeavoured to avoid contact with the deputy, and he did not initiate contact with me.

That occasion showed a different side to Reg. When I became quiet and thoughtful, not really responding to the impassioned speakers, he put his arm around me and whispered,

'What is the matter? Do you want to go home?'

Such concern in his voice and the realisation he was about to forgo the after-party that was planned made me shrug off the dread in my gut and quickly reply,

'No, of course not!'

Another warning that I overlooked, this man really cared for me. So we went to the party at the pub, and I endeavoured to get lost in the crowd, anxiously scanning the faces for the one man I wanted to avoid. But the die had been cast, and I was too naive to see it. The following April Easter holiday was going to change my life forever.

Haiku: Inspired, so committed; Ready to save the whole world; Sudden danger, fall.

CHAPTER 20

Easter 1962 – My First Driving Lesson

IT WAS THE EASTER term holidays, and my boyfriend had promised to teach me to drive his car, a 1938 Chevrolet, immaculately presented and lovingly cared for. I'd had a few instructions in changing the floor-based gears while standing still, and an actual drive was promised for the first fine day of the holidays. Tuesday dawned sunny and clear, so we drove into town, parked in Elizabeth Street, as you could in 1962, and walked to the GIO building in Martin Place to get the car comprehensively insured as at that stage, the car only had third-party property. Reg asked if the insurance began instantly and was assured that was the case. Otherwise, the driving lesson would have been postponed until the following day. So off to Centennial Park we went, brand-new L plates on, and I had my first drive. There were very few cars travelling around the park, and my confidence grew in leaps and bounds; I was driving at a very sedate pace of 15mph. Increasing speed to 25mph, I drove out into the nearest suburb and, with some difficulty, parked for us to get lunch and then back into the park to practise reversing and parking. I was doing so well, Reg said, 'Time to go home, you can drive'.

Fatal mistake. It was now nearing 3pm, traffic had increased considerably, and I was keeping pace with other cars, now travelling at 30mph. I had no idea where I was, just relying on my navigator: straight ahead, left at the next. Unfortunately, he had not given enough lead warning or uttered the important words 'Brake first' when suddenly, there was the road and horror of horrors, a car was in the middle of the road, trying to turn right.

Still, full of confidence, I did as I had been told and, without slowing, turned the wheel hard left. Too late, I realised I was about to hit the stationary car and instead of instinctively braking, I froze, wheel on full lock and foot still on the accelerator. The grand old Chevie broadsided the car in the middle of the road and then nosed between two parked cars, sending each into its neighbour, and finally endeavoured to heave itself up onto the footpath, fortunately failing and settling down in the gutter.

A crowd gathered, the police arrived, Reg was trying to placate the furious driver, I was having an anxiety asthma attack, and a passing nurse was helping me breathe. She decided an ambulance wasn't necessary; someone supplied an inhaler, and as the Chevy was a little battered but still definitely drivable, unlike two of the other cars, we drove away.

First stop a pub. Reg needed a drink to recover from the shock of his pride and joy being battered, and he decided I needed a drink to calm my shattered nerves. I think he had heard brandy is good for such cases and ordered me a Brandy Alexander, being the female equivalent to medicinal brandy.

That really was my undoing. I hadn't been much of a drinker, a beer shandy in hot weather or a Pimms on social occasions. I have to admit, I didn't mind the creamy taste, but then the outpouring of emotion, floods of tears, sobbing, hiccupping, more sobbing. Reg took me home, and as my flat mate had gone home to spend Easter with her parents, he put me to bed and stayed with me through the night, stroking my hair, holding me tight.

When morning light dawned, I surrendered my virginity.

CHAPTER 21

The Morning After

SO HOW DID I feel when I awoke a newly deflowered woman? Madly in love, anxious to rush back to my lover's arms and do it over and over again?

Not at all. The overriding sensation as I snuggled deeper under my doona was one of impending doom. First problem: I had broken the primal rule of the boarding house, no males allowed in bedrooms. My lover had slipped away at early light so he wouldn't be caught, but I had a hazy recollection of hours of heartbreaking sobbing and strangled words of woe that would certainly have been heard by others in the house and probably by anyone in the street. Another sensation flooded me: humiliation. I was never one to cry, not even when the baby lamb died or the cat was run over. I had no explanation for last night's behaviour. So I probably faced having to find new lodgings.

Second even bigger problem: The sex I had just had was unprotected; I could right now be pregnant! This was definitely not the plan I had for my life. I was only a trainee teacher and would not gain my teaching certificate for three bonded years. I could well imagine an unmarried pregnant trainee teacher would be given her marching orders, probably having to pay back the cost of the university education I had enjoyed.

I was not even ready to fall in love. I had witnessed the transformation of my former flat mate, who, when she really fell in love with her boyfriend, avoided all other social contact, wanting to be only with him. There was no more going to check out a new dance hall, wine bar or live music at a pub with girlfriends; she wanted only a definite twosome. Then I remembered catching up with two school friends, both pushing prams and unable to hold a conversation about anything but babies. I was definitely not ready for that. I had told my mother, some years before, in a fit of temper, 'I am never going to have children. I am over that because I have raised five of yours'.

I hadn't even thought of the legal ramifications of causing an accident that had damaged five cars. Enough to say I was overwhelmed by the thought that I had lost my lodgings, my career and my whole life plan.

The next reaction was one of anger. I felt betrayed. Why on earth did he let me drive home in real traffic? Why hadn't he given better instructions, been able to grab the wheel or done something to stop the car? Why had he fed me alcohol to break down my defences? Why did he take advantage of me and leave me in this mess?

Once I became angry, I was stirred into action. First, get the local paper and find new lodgings. Done, I found a retired lady who wanted to rent a bedroom with use of kitchen, bath and laundry to a quiet single lady. I would move in on the weekend. I wrote a letter to my landlady saying that I had decided to move back home.

The threat of pregnancy was a little more difficult. I had no idea of my menstrual cycle; I didn't have any problems and hadn't had this situation before. I would just have to wait and see. Saying goodbye to Reg shouldn't be a problem now that I was fired with a resolution to save my independent lifestyle, and I was never going to drive a car again anyway.

While I spent the day planning my new life, my boyfriend spent the day finding people to fix his car. He must have thought he was very kind-hearted and generous, willing to pay for all repairs that I had caused and still happy to see me. He was totally unprepared for the vengeful vixen that he met that evening. I had been building up a steam of fury all day and let him have full vent.

'That car accident was your fault as much as mine as you were the teacher in charge. I should never had been driving in real traffic. You took advantage of me, and now I cannot stay here. I am moving back home. Also, I might be pregnant, as you didn't take any precautions, and if so, I will lose my job as well. I really regret what happened yesterday, all of it, and I don't want to see you ever again'.

Shock, hurt and panic all registered on his face as he tried to put his arms around me.

'Please, I just want to take care of you. I'll marry you. Please don't turn away'.

For a moment, our eyes met, and I registered the pain in his soft brown eyes and saw the traces of tears in the corners. That struck a chord within me, and I knew the only way I could leave him was if I moved away and didn't see him again. Well, I had a few weeks to discover if I really was pregnant, so I would wait a little longer, and then, if I was released from this fear, I could move rapidly. In the meantime, we would not go there again.

I still felt compelled to leave the boarding house, so the following weekend, I moved in with the lady who wanted a quiet soul as a boarder. Her house was located at Enmore, which meant an extra bus ride to Strathfield station, but I was determined to become a totally dedicated teacher and disappear from my lover's life.

I visited my horse to say goodbye and told Wendy that I would be happy to sell him to her. Thus, another chapter of my life ended. It was like saying goodbye to my childhood, all those years where horses had dominated. Work would now be my passion; there was to be no place for love. Frantically, I threw myself into lesson preparation, strict as a monk avoiding earthly temptation.

My first day back at school, at 3.30pm, there was the battered Chevy in the car park. I avoided leaving with the others and stayed in the staffroom until the car went. Finally, I ventured out to catch the train.

The following day, the Chevy was at the station, waiting for me at 8.30am.

'I can't stop. I'm on playground duty', I shouted, running up the street.

'I will be here at 3.30, and I won't leave until you talk to me' was the reply as he drove alongside me. So I had the day to prepare,

MAUREEN ANNE MORGAN

be strong, not get in the car and just tell him I didn't ever want to
see him again.

At 3.30, a taxi was waiting just in case the Chevy held bad
memories. I waited until all the teachers and students had left, but
then the cleaners were very interested in the taxi that was waiting
such a long time, so I went and got in the back seat and said,

'Take me to Blacktown station, please, driver'.

'Let's have a quiet coffee and chat, and then I will take you
anywhere you want to go' was his reply, so we drove to a little
coffee shop near Parramatta Park, and after ordering, Reg dropped
his bombshell.

'I have left my wife, and it is for good this time. She has said she
will never take me back and that it will take all my money to keep
paying for the house and for her children. So I will not be able to
support you and your baby, if there is one, as well.

'I couldn't lie to her. When she saw the car, she knew something
was wrong. I think she is better off without me. She is quite pretty,
and maybe she will find another man who will love her as she
deserves to be loved. But that man isn't me, and I don't want to
pretend anymore. I have taken a room in Marrickville, so if you
really don't want to know me, I will be out of your area'.

That really took the wind out of my sails. I suddenly needed a
cigarette, the first time I had actually needed one. I had taken up
smoking at university to appear more sophisticated than I really
was. All my assurances about our friendship not endangering his
marriage came crashing down about my ears. In fact, I was truly to
blame for his leaving home. I had encouraged the friendship, and our
banter was naturally flirtatious. By asking him to teach me to drive,
I had set in motion the events that had led to our coupling, and by
my recriminations, I had made him feel responsible for me and my
possible predicament. Everything pointed to my grave responsibility
in dispossessing a wife of her husband and children of their father.
I felt like a penitent monk seeking self-flagellation to repent for my
sins.

92

I was at a loss for words, and when 'I am so sorry' struggled from my mouth, tears poured from my eyes as well. I couldn't shrug off his arm around me, and when I saw he was weeping too, I just dissolved in hurt and grief. Fortunately, we were in a dark corner of the café, or embarrassment would have defeated that very precious moment.

Finally, he said, 'Look, let's wait a while to see if you really are pregnant. I promise I won't touch you again, and if you are pregnant, I will look after you. If not, you need never see me again', which was, in fact, close to the very plan I had devised earlier. Just in case though, I asked him to take me to Parramatta station, not home. He would only see me at school at the end of a working day.

That night, I shed more tears, thinking about him leaving his children and my guilty part in that. Also, l was troubled by his obvious distress at not seeing me again when he had given up so much. Added to this was the overwhelming need to feel his comforting arms around me and to hear his assurance he would always care for me.

During the following month, that sense of impending doom never left me. Was it possible to realise the exact moment when you conceive? The sex that I'd experience had been a mixture of excitement and pain, not the overwhelming rush of love in every romance novel. I had been somewhat concerned with the shuddering, gasping male who lay on me, fearing he might expire from a heart attack. I had heard stories about such a calamity from nurses where I had worked. I had also heard stories about girls falling pregnant on their first sexual encounter as if that was nature's plan. Did my fear encourage me to believe I was pregnant, a fear that grew with each passing week?

Once a week, the taxi arrived at 3.30, and we would repeat the original performance, coffee at Parramatta, no deliverance from fear, holding hands, tearful goodbye at the station.

Then at seven one Sunday morning, the taxi arrived at the nursing home where I still worked the Saturday night shift. This was week 5 without a reassuring showing, and I was tired and fearful. Reg drove me home, and we sat in the car planning our next move. First a visit to the doctor and he would come with me. Then we should find a place to live together, preferably Strathfield, convenient for my two jobs. He would work seven days a week, if necessary, to cover expenses, and I would work as long as possible to save for future difficult days.

He told me that his mother-in-law was living with her daughter to look after the children while their mother now went to work at the local club and that his wife was now enjoying a new social life with work colleagues and seemed much happier.

'I should have left years ago for her sake', he mused.

He also mentioned the insurance company was refusing to honour the policy on the basis that it didn't start until sundown! He had received threatening letters from two of the five drivers involved.

'Not your worry', he said, 'it was my car that did the damage'. Yes, but it had been me behind the wheel!

During my teenage years, my regular GP had been a Dr O'Brien, a Catholic with conservative views and also was GP to my entire family. Not the right doctor for this occasion. So together with the prospective father, I visited another GP in Burwood and was officially declared pregnant, possible date due January 1963.

Even though Reg had sworn he would marry me, it was not going to be possible for at least two years as there had to be a separation of at least twelve months before one can apply for divorce. So now I was faced with what would the Education Department do with me?

CHAPTER 22

Fateful Decision

HOWEVER, THE BURWOOD DOCTOR had offered another solution. He wrote a referral to a clinic in Bondi that would do a termination at a cost of eighty pounds if I went there within the next three weeks.

What a moral dilemma! If my mother had taken this remedy for her predicament, I would never have been born, and though at the time I was probably wishing exactly that, I could see the irony in the situation. However, she had a mother who could look after her baby while she worked. My mother still had five children at home, one of whom was severely disabled. My mother had completed her training and could continue to work in her profession; I had barely started and would be unable to continue. I don't think I really wrestled with the criminal morality of taking a prospective life. This was the 1960s, when even children knew about the senseless destruction of life in war and women demanded the freedom to choose what to do with their bodies and opposed conservative men who still wanted to banish them to the kitchen and nursery.

Reg had been discussing the problem with his cab driver friends, and his best mate, Ray Fisher, agreed to pay the total cost, if I would agree.

So I accepted Ray's kind offer, and Reg and I, on a cold rainy day, visited the doctor's surgery underneath the cliffs of south Bondi. I was strapped into a dentist-type chair, my legs raised high and feet placed in handcuff-type stirrups. No anaesthetic or tranquiliser of any kind, as a nurse forced open my vagina with a steel trap. Then a suitably gowned and scrubbed doctor pushed a long-handled extractor into my womb and removed the growing foetus.

'Would you like to see it?' he asked and pushed a steel Petri dish under my nose. In the midst of blood and fluid, I saw this embryo, like a big-headed tadpole, before it was flushed away.

I was handed a packet of antibiotics to take and advised to see my local GP to have a D and C.

'Just tell him you had a bad bleed and think you have lost the baby. You can even tell him what it looked like coming away'.

So that was the reason for the forced viewing.

Reg and I sat in the car, facing the cold grey sea, and wept. He was probably thinking that could have been the son he had always wanted, and I was thinking, what if one day I want a child and cannot have one.

Now was the time to make the decision. Do I follow through and determine never to see this man again? He has promised to respect my decision and keep away, but here we are, locked in each other's arms, our tears mingling, united in pain and grief for the child we might have had. The connection was so strong. We had the same leftish views on peace and justice; we liked the same music, had read the same books and made each other laugh and cry; and I was so guilt-ridden about what I had done to destroy his happiness.

Suddenly, moving in together seemed definitely the right thing to do. Both of us would work hard to pay expenses. I would go to the doctor, organise my D and C and get the miracle pill I had heard about to prevent any future pregnancy. I would dedicate my life to making sure his girls had a wonderful relationship with their father and would one day make peace with his wife.

So clear was this mantra inside my head that I failed to see that it meant giving up my freedom and the plans I once had for my future.

To retrace the origins of these plans, firstly, I had planned to compete in three-day events with my wonderful horse Rajah. As a teacher, I had hoped to be posted to the country where I would meet other horse enthusiasts. While living in Chullora, I had a horse-mad friend called Livia, who at the age of sixteen had run off to join a buckjumping show that travelled around the country. She would drop me a postcard when she was in a big town, with an invite to come and join her. Sometimes I would dream of doing just that. Now horses were right out of the picture.

Then there were the three best friends from high school days, Janice, Margaret and Pat. We had made a pact that we would celebrate our combined twenty-first birthdays (we were all born in November) in Trafalgar Square, UK. All were still in touch and planning the trip. I could see that saving to go overseas was now out of the question.

Finally, I had made two significant friends at the high school, Ann, who had just returned from tripping overseas, and Trisha, who was saving to go there. Together, we would seek out interesting music venues and dance halls as none of us were involved with a male. Now I was totally involved with someone most unsuitable, and I could see that all the money I earned would be spent paying the costs of the accident.

Here once again, when I had done something unimaginably bad, my incredible luck smiled on me. I was still working Saturday nights at the nursing home, and one of the more lucid ladies liked to chat as I washed her. She noticed I was not my usual cheerful self and asked what was troubling me. Eventually, I told her the whole car crash story, which she found hilarious. Then I included the fact that the insurance company were refusing to pay the claims so I would have to. Immediately, she became very serious and said, 'This is just not right. You would not have been driving if you had not been insured. I will speak to my son about this'.

True to her word, she did, having asked me to write down all the details of the incident. Apparently, her son was a high-ranking official with GIO. Within a relatively short time, the insurance company had a change of mind, and the demanding letters ceased.

I was so relieved and thought that would be the end of my car crash troubles. Not quite, but that story deserves another chapter.

CHAPTER 23

My Brush with the Law

THE WHEELS OF JUSTICE ground very slowly but surely. It must have been term 3, and I was in the midst of describing the wonders of ancient Rome when a pupil knocked at my door. She was the daily messenger based in the office, and she had a note from the headmaster.

'You are urgently required at the office. Please set your class some work to do and tell them I will be along shortly to supervise'. Signed by the headmaster.

This was most unusual. I had never known the boss to supervise students, maybe the deputy, but never the boss. A closer look at the messenger, I noticed she could barely conceal her excitement. What on earth was happening!

Quickly, I devised an exercise to write ten questions about ancient Rome with answers and then told them the headmaster was coming to hear their responses.

Down the hall, into the foyer, I passed the secretaries, also goggle-eyed with excitement.

I knocked on the headmaster's closed door and went in to meet two large policemen, who stood when I entered. The headmaster also stood and said, 'These gentlemen want to speak with you in private, so I will go along and supervise your class'.

I guess I too must be goggle-eyed by now and frantically thinking, 'Has someone died? Have I broken the law?' I reddened as I remembered abortion was illegal (as it still is in NSW some fifty-five years later). Had I been found out?

Then the senior officer spoke. 'Maureen Vinnard, did you, in April of this year, reside at 56 Aldeen St Strathfield?'

'Yes', I mumbled.

He continued, 'And were you, on April 22nd, driving a 1938 Chevrolet sedan, licence number BJ112, that was involved in an accident at the corner of Cleveland St and Dawson Rd, Matraville?'

'I didn't know where it was, but yes, that was the car, and I was driving'.

'Well, we are here to serve you with an infringement notice, that of negligent driving. It has been somewhat difficult to track you down. You have failed to supply current residential address with your employer'.

'I just forgot. I would have done it next year when we all fill in the forms again'.

'But unfortunately, you had an accident this year. You are required to attend court on the date stated. This date has already been adjourned once, so you cannot seek another'.

'What if I can't get to court?'

'You will be found guilty and sentenced in your absence. Do you have any proof of your current address?'

'No, not on me. I don't carry bills around'.

'Well, I suggest you take a proof of residence to your local police station, show this notice and make sure you do that within four working days from now. We don't want to chase you up here again. Make sure you rectify your place of residence with your employer today'.

With that, they both turned and walked out. Red faced and close to tears, I crept out, past the inquisitive eyes of the secretaries and school messenger, back to my classroom.

'Good work, class, you know plenty about Ancient Rome' was the headmaster's parting remarks to the class, and then with his back turned to them, he muttered to me, 'See me at lunchtime'.

That was an embarrassing meeting as he was furious that I had shown him to be unaware of the basic legal requirements of record-keeping in the school.

God, if he only knew I had changed address three times in two terms and what other crimes I had committed while under his rule.

Now I had the problem of proving my address. Caught up in a whirlwind of guilt over the car crash, end of the pregnancy and overwhelming love and desire for the man who had vowed to stand by me come what may, I had recently moved in with him to a flat in Burwood, which, of course, was leased in his name. In desperation after the meeting with the headmaster, I gave my address as that of my parents. Now I had to tell them about the negligent driving charge, which meant telling them about the car accident. I could pretend I didn't want to worry the single lady I boarded with by asking her to sign an affidavit. The infringement notice proved my original Strathfield address, and I had told my parents about moving in with this lovely retired lady. Then the confession that the new boyfriend had been teaching me to drive and I had an accident. My parents were aghast; neither of them could drive and couldn't see why I needed to; didn't I live near a station and catch a train to work? After another lecture about the dangers of driving a car, to which I agreed wholeheartedly, and the danger of now having a criminal conviction which could affect my career, to which I replied the headmaster knows and has not suspended me, they agreed to sign the affidavit in front of a JP, which I took to the local police station.

I didn't attend court and received notification of my penalty. The offence was to be recorded against my future licence, and a one-hundred-pound fine had been imposed. I didn't think I would ever drive a car, so apart from continuing to work every Saturday night to pay the fine, I was untroubled.

Reg and I had moved to a room with a shared bathroom and laundry facilities in Station St, Burwood, and yes, I was truly, madly, deeply in love. I no longer went jockeying in the taxi, but sometimes he would collect me and take me to tea with his cab driver mates. I paid the rent; he gave half his earnings to his wife. Every second Sunday, he would collect the two eldest girls and take them for a ride to the beach or the mountains or Sydney Botanical Gardens while I slept. Eventually, the baby demanded that she wanted to go too, so I joined them and worked every second Saturday night. Those were wonderful days. I loved being with the girls, and they seemed to like me too. Finally, I met Marge, the wife, and considering my history, she was very nice to me. She had met another man, Lionel, and seemed very happy with her new life. After her mum died, she, Lionel and the girls moved to the coast, where she really enjoyed life by the sea.

CHAPTER 24

New Friends, New Experiences

IT'S FUNNY HOW WHEN you become a couple, life changes dramatically. His friends become your friends, and you see more of them than your own friends. Reg, a cab driver, had three fellow driver buddies, Ray Fisher, John Morgan and Peter Deville. Interestingly, the former two became my would-be lovers, and one of the two would become my second husband. Ray Fisher was a lean, intense young man with deep-set brown eyes and a mop of unruly brown hair. A self-taught academic, he was widely read, a communist in philosophy, with a deep interest in astronomy and archaeology. He was also a polished dancer and ice skater and considered a wise sage by his friends. Unattached, he was the perfect platonic friend who continued my philosophical education, held my hand ice skating and swirled me around the dance floor at the Russian club we frequented. He also encouraged us to join archaeological digs in the Royal National Park at Audley. This is where I met Ray's friends, Kay Stephens, her daughter Jill, son-in-law Douglas, and suitor Victor Leuliette. We took picnics to the national park and joined in the digs. Later, Kay and Vic bought a house in Bundeena, and we were able to spend weekends there. Kay was a staunch feminist, having divorced her husband and raised her two daughters alone. She was outgoing and energetic, loved bush walking and canoeing and was very active in the Ban the Bomb campaigns. Her younger daughter, Brenda, had trained as a nurse and was overseas at this time. The older girl, Jill, was a social worker, her husband Douglas was a teacher, and they lived in Seaforth in a house belonging to the Main Roads Department, part of a parcel of land earmarked for the new harbour crossing and connecting freeway. This, of course, was never built, and Reg and I inherited the house when Douglas was transferred to Wollongong.

John Morgan lived with his wife, Val, and three children, Ian, Bruce and daughter, Lee, in Fairlight. John was definitely a ladies' man, and his eldest son followed in his footsteps. On our first meeting, I distinctly had the feeling of both of them undressing me with their eyes. Val was a lovely, quiet lady and Lee a noisy ten-year-old. Their house was an old-fashioned two-storey, a walking distance from the bay. John had a passion for Manly, where he had lived since his birth, leaving for a short stay in Burke where his father owned the wool scour and then travelling overseas during World War Two with the Royal Air Force. As a teenager, he had worked at the kiosk at Manly Pool, where at age ten, I had bought scallops and boiling water to make tea for my family.

Peter Deville was an attractive Frenchman living in Frenchs Forest with his wife, Yvonne, and three little girls. Reg and I spent a weekend there, and I remember cuddling the baby and rocking her to sleep, filled with remorse at my actions with my never-to-be-born baby. Sadly, baby Babette contracted pneumonia and passed away shortly afterwards. My strongest recollection of Peter is his great respect for food. In my experience, salad meant shredded lettuce, sliced tomato and cucumber on a plate with tinned beetroot, mayonnaise, a slice of Kraft Cheese, maybe a boiled egg and always white sliced bread. Peter's simple salad was a major project. He took extreme care in preparing the wooden salad bowl, wiping with olive oil and a touch of garlic. The lettuce was torn in pieces, tomatoes chopped in chunks and cucumber with the skin still on and other ingredients such as avocado, olives and red onion were added. The dressing was always hand mixed, and different cheeses, such as camembert and blue vein, were served on a board. The bread was dark rye, and a glass of wine, usually red, was a standard part of every meal. His potato salad, featuring mashed boiled eggs and dill without mayonnaise, was a masterpiece that I endeavoured to copy but was never as successful. A year or so later, Yvonne left Peter and went to live with her mother in Thirroul. Peter met Margaret at a YMCA hostel in Sydney, and we remain the best of friends today.

During my single days, I loved to dance, not only doing it, but also watching professionals, especially from overseas. I remember watching the Georgian dancers, the men with their athletic leaps and the girls who seem to float across the floor, never showing movement in their feet. Another memorable performance, whose place of origin I have forgotten, starred a male dancer performing as a deer. He had exquisite control of his body and movement. The taut muscle of a nervous animal ready to flee, the shiver of anticipation, the extended nostril, the quivering neck, just beauty in motion. If I close my eyes, I can still picture that performance today. How I would love to have conveyed my thanks to that artist; he left me with a magical moment and a memory I would take to my grave.

There was a darker side to my relationship with Reg. He must have been having a difficult time, only seeing his daughters every second weekend, perhaps having second thoughts about leaving them, having no formal educational achievements compared with my university-trained friends and probably not being totally sure I would stay with him. Anyone who can get rid of a baby would probably be happy to abandon a mate if the circumstances proved favourable. I had left my job at the nursing home and begun working behind the bar at a hotel in Belfield. A friend of mine from pony club days was working there and told me they were training young girls. The hours were less, the pay was better, and being able to sleep at night was a definite bonus. Reg would drive me to work and pick me up afterwards and didn't seem to mind. But Saturday night became stripper night. A beautiful young girl would be led in by her bikie-type boyfriend and would slowly strip to the seductive tune from the sound system. She seemed to me to be in a daze. I couldn't see how the entire performance could be erotic as she seemed totally removed from the experience. But the punters loved it, and the beer and the tips flowed. I can remember thinking, 'I am safe here behind the bar', but I wouldn't have been allowed on the other side as this was a public bar and women weren't allowed in; they had to use the ladies' bar (or pigpen). Then the boss asked me to wear fishnet stockings and black shorts and sell cigarettes throughout the bar while the show took place as the drinkers were too busy watching to order more drinks. I did this twice, and then my boyfriend demanded I leave.

I couldn't believe a man, not my boss, was telling me what to do. I hadn't had this happen since I was fourteen. I was not happy with the new arrangement at the hotel but was not about to be told by someone else what to do about it. I can't remember the first time I felt threatened by him, but I am sure it had something to do with insisting it was my right to make decisions about my life.

The first violent encounter was after the Russian Ball held at Sydney Town Hall. It was a fancy-dress affair, and Reg and I went as school kids, he in short pants, long socks, shirt and tie and me in my school uniform, fishnet black stockings and hair in plaits. We had a great time eating, drinking and dancing, but Reg wasn't a keen dancer, so I spent most of the time on the floor with Ray. As Ray led me back to the table, another young man asked if I wanted to dance, and without a thought, I said yes, and he whirled me onto the floor. It so happened that this was the last bracket of the night, and after three fast numbers, there was the slow, smoochy goodnight number. I excused myself and headed back to our group. Reg had obviously had too much to drink, and John and Val were having words with him. Ray, Kay and Vic were leaving, and I ran to them to say goodbye. When I came back, John was forcing Reg to his feet and saying, 'I am putting you into a taxi to go home'. Val put her arms around me and said, 'Why don't you come home with us, leave him to sleep it off, go home tomorrow'.

Obviously, they knew something about my partner's behaviour that I did not, but with all the confidence of a naive, first-love affair girl, I refused.

Such an unworldly girl was I, having never seen my stepfather lay a hand on my mother, his children yes, but never his wife, I couldn't believe this man, who swore he loved me to distraction would ever harm me, so I blithely said, 'That's okay, I'll put him to bed, but it would probably be better for us to find a taxi'.

John was still holding Reg and Val me as we left the Town Hall and found a taxi very quickly. Reg was extremely quiet during the ride home and didn't ask about the fare that I paid with the ten pounds John had forced into my hand. Once inside, Reg let fly with the most vicious outpouring about me being a slut, ready to run off with anyone who asked me. Then he hit me in the face with such force, he broke my tooth.

Shock and horror engulfed me as I slid to the floor, holding my mouth. Reg, in turn, overwhelmed with shock and horror at what he had done, gathered me in his arms, whispering, 'I'm so sorry, so sorry'.

But the damage had been done. To the tooth that needed replacing by a partial plate and to my belief in love that would never harm and always protect. I felt a distancing, a mistrust, but unfortunately, no lessoning of the love I felt for this man, who now held me, caressed me and whispered he loved me.

As the weeks passed, I had a strange new resolve. I had to leave this man but could only do that by making him want to leave me. How crazy does that sound now! I had such a feeling of lack of self-worth, possibly engendered by seeking the abortion, that I felt it would only be a matter of time before Reg realised what a hideous person I was and would be happy to leave me. My self-esteem was so low that I reasoned if he hurt me before he left, that would only be my just desserts, having caused him to leave his wife and children and lose a prospective son and an immaculate car. There have been a few occasions in my life when I distinctly remember wanting to die. In this case, I was rather expecting that could happen.

All this before I turned twenty-one!

I had stopped working at the hotel as Reg wouldn't drive me there and public transport was unavailable. Although as a bonded teacher, working outside the profession was illegal, finances were tight, so I found work in the saloon bar at the hotel near Town Hall station. This was to cause some concern the following year, when I was invited to a fellow teacher's home for the engagement of her nineteen-year-old daughter, Candy. Imagine my horror when, on introduction to her fiancé, I recognised the naval officer who had frequented the hotel and had constantly chatted me up. Even worse, he knew my face and kept repeating,

'I am sure I know you from somewhere'. Fortunately, he didn't connect the barmaid and the teacher, so I said, 'Well, I must have a double out there'.

CHAPTER 25

November 1962 – My Memorable Twenty-First Birthday

AS MY TWENTY-FIRST BIRTHDAY neared, I made another momentous decision. This would be my moment of truth when I would force this man to leave me. My birthday was on a Sunday. I worked Saturday nights, and my family expected me home for a birthday lunch on Sunday. Reg didn't seem particularly interested in this big event in my life, so I told him I would spend the weekend at my parents and would be home on Sunday evening. On the Saturday, I planned to tell work I was sick and have a big night out clubbing with my good friend Deidre from horse-riding days. Did I really expect to meet another love of my life in a single night on the town?

I had made my plans, forgetting that a school environment knows everything about you. Two weeks before the date, I was asked what I intended to do for my big night, and when I said go dancing with a girlfriend and her boyfriend, a fellow teacher said, 'I can line you up with a really nice guy to go dancing with, and I'll come too with my boyfriend'. So I agreed. Deidre was happy to drop the idea, and Janelle waxed lyrical about this lovely fellow who had been dumped by his fiancé, who had left to go overseas. What I hadn't worked out was where I would sleep during the early hours of Sunday morning until it was a reasonable hour to turn up at my parents' home. I had wanted to drink champagne at dawn at some late-night club in town and hadn't thought much beyond that.

The new guy was a great dancer, and we had a wonderful time at the Trocodero and then onto Kings Cross, where I danced and drank far too much. My blind date was a lovely man, who felt I should be driven home and so hailed a taxi and asked me for an address. Now

I felt obliged to say my parents' address in Greenacre as this was my address at school and I hadn't told anyone about my boyfriend, much less living with him.

So at about 2am, we arrived at Keira Ave, and he wanted to walk me to the door.

'No, don't keep the taxi waiting. Thank you for making my birthday so special'. A quick goodnight kiss and hug and I headed for the house next door, closer to the paddock where I intended to hide out until a respectable hour.

For the second time in my life, I discovered the hour before dawn is the coldest time of night, and this time, I didn't have a blanket, only a jacket. Fortunately, the house was still deserted and the barn, water and dew proof, so I huddled in the corner, waiting for morning. I hadn't told my parents about working at the pub, rightly guessing they wouldn't approve, and what they didn't know wouldn't worry them. For the same reason, neither had I told them about moving in with my boyfriend. Once the sun was high and I had warmed up a little and cleaned myself with a hanky and water from the still working tap, I walked to my parents' house and was greeted with open arms and the familiar smell of the Sunday roast cooking.

Late in the afternoon, it was time to go home, so with some trepidation, I made my way back to Station St, Burwood. No one was at home, so I busied myself with preparation to teach in the morning. Later that evening, Reg arrived, the smell of beer on his breath as he grabbed me and hissed into my face, 'Who were you with last night?'

'Out with my friends from school, celebrating my twenty-first birthday, as you weren't interested'.

Defiance was probably not a good move, I thought, as my head thudded against the wall.

'You're nothing but a slut, a whore, an XXX bitch', he said with hands around my throat and slamming my head into the wall.

Stupidly, inwardly, I was agreeing with him, thinking, 'Will you kill me or just leave me?' Finally, he threw me onto the floor and stormed out. He didn't return that night, and in the morning, I had to put on make-up to cover the bruise on my face and wear a scarf to cover the redness of my neck. I bought a paper to find new accommodation, feeling relieved I had survived what I thought could be my final hour on earth.

The following night, I had packed my belongings, although I had still not found suitable lodgings. Maybe I could go back to my parents for the four weeks until the Christmas holidays. Maybe I should have gone there that afternoon because the following night, Reg was back. So contrite, so apologetic. 'Why did I lose my temper? How could I hurt the one I love so much? What can I do to make it right?' This was not the response I had anticipated, and here I was, melting under the anguished look in his eyes. Oh well, looks like I'm in for the long haul after all.

CHAPTER 26

April 1966 — Love and Marriage

REG KEPT HIS PROMISE and never raised his hand against me again. Instead, he smashed crockery, destroyed walls and even kicked his car when the black clouds of anger engulfed him. He worked longer shifts and encouraged me to repeat my failed university subject at night, which I did successfully. I had spent the first year of the school holidays attending courses to train to be a school librarian. There wasn't a degree course in those days; teachers who were librarians taught classes as well and had one period a day to do library administration work, that is ordering, classifying and keeping accounts. The invaluable library assistant who could type made all the cards and kept borrowing records and, in her spare time, covered books. The library was in the top floor of our unfinished building, and when that was finished, a starter library of about four hundred nonfiction and five hundred fiction books, plus a set of encyclopaedias, was delivered. This was where the ladies of the canteen were invaluable, spending their afternoons covering books.

I loved teaching and became involved in extracurricular activities, coaching the basketball team and, with the very talented English master, helping to organise a talent night. One of the book-covering ladies worked at Jansen's factory, and she made possible the loan of a dozen 1930s swimming costumes which, with music teacher Chris on piano, formed the basis of a musical review.

Later that year, when the hall was completed, we held our first disco, and even though I had asked the local police to drive by, it needed most of the male staff, armed with softball bats, to stand at the gates and keep the hoons at bay. Also, by the end of that year, I found my two bosom buddies; Ann and Trish were both in steady relationships and considering marriage.

In 1966, Reg's divorce came through, his wife married her beau, and Reg proposed to me. By this time, we were living in Summer Hill, sharing half a house with one elderly lady. My landlady, who lived in the other half of the house, was most surprised one day to meet my fifteen-year-old sister, who, having run away from home, was hoping to stay with her big sister. Margaret returned home and kept the secret that Maureen was now living with her boyfriend.

First, break the news to my family that I am actually marrying this most unsuitable man, and if they want to come to the registry office on 22 April, they can witness the event. All except my stepfather that is. I was adamant that I did not want him to attend. I didn't need someone to give me away; I was twenty-four, a grown woman making her own choice, and knowing that he didn't approve, I didn't want him there, full stop. Mum didn't really approve either, but she knew I was determined to make this happen, and she wanted to support my decision and wish me luck. On Saturday, 22 April, Reg's birthday, he and I and a handful of friends and relatives went to the registry office to be wed. Horror of horrors, the ceremony was a very formal affair where the presiding officer in a ringing voice read out, 'Reginald Ray Mahoney of Prospect Rd, Summer Hill, do you take Maureen Anne Vinnard of Prospect Rd, Summer Hill, to be your lawfully wedded wife?'

There it was out in the open, to my mother, my English master and my best friends, from whom I had kept it a secret for four years. I was very red-faced as I said 'I do'.

We went to Ray's flat in Bondi for afternoon tea and cut the cake that Trisha's mum had made for me, and that evening, everyone went to dinner at Anna's European restaurant in Kings Cross. I was back at school on Monday.

CHAPTER 27

1967 — Birth of My First Baby

SOMEHOW, YOU CAN'T CONTROL human nature. I had gone from the seventeen-year-old girl who had told her mother in a fit of temper, 'I am never going to have any children. I have done my bit by raising five of yours', to a twenty-five-year-old woman who desperately wanted a baby. Not just one, but two, spaced apart of course. Please don't let me be like my mother and have twins! I just didn't want a lonely only child, as I had been for seven years.

If you want to have two children by the age of thirty, you should be pregnant by the age of twenty-five. Planning was of the upmost importance. The necessary prerequisites were in place, marriage and a house with a big backyard and a nice neighbourhood school within walking distance. A slight amendment to the original plan meant I was still completing the last unit of my degree. Falling in love, whirlwind romance and the wedding having upset my study routine, but nothing that could not be overcome. After all, if women in Asia only pause in their back-breaking work in the fields to stop and have a baby, why would completing assignments and sitting an exam stop me? I would be taking maternity leave from my full-time job in the last month, so it should be a breeze.

I wanted a September baby. Most animals reproduce in the spring to enable offspring to get fat in the summer and be ready to survive the winter chills. Therefore, I was most put out when, come the new year, I was not pregnant. Frantically, I launched into 'get pregnant or die in the attempt' as I wanted to avoid being heavily pregnant when the December heat began and feared having a child with a birthday close to Xmas Day. The diet and exercise regime were already in place. I had given up horse riding, smoking and alcohol and was filled with virtue and zeal to produce the perfect baby. My husband must have been worn ragged with my constant demands for sex and must have heaved a sigh of relief when the purpose was achieved. I had already contacted an old school friend who worked at the maternity hospital to advise me on the best gynaecologist available, so all was in place.

The first four months were a breeze. I shrugged off morning sickness, lost the taste for tea and coffee and demanded my cravings for strawberries and pineapple be met, although both fruits were out of season. My devoted husband proved indefatigable in searching for my every desire. Concentrating on assignments for my psychology course proved more difficult as I was more interested in reading about birth defects and how to avoid them. Then it became difficult to fit behind the wheel of the car and impossible to take a double-period lesson without needing to rush to the ladies, and running for the train was out of the question.

I was falling behind again in my study regimen. Assignments just got there in time, but I didn't feel confident I was on top of the work. I looked forward to maternity leave when I would have nothing to do but concentrate on catching up.

The last day at school was a little emotional, even though I was just taking a year off to bond with my baby and organise my life to be able to get back to work.

The cards and presents from the children struck a chord that my automated buying what was needed for a baby had not. They seemed more excited about the fact that I was about to give birth than I was. Older members of staff who had tried to advise me, saying, 'It will be a whole new world for you', made me feel uneasy.

I had planned down to the last detail. I was a teacher for goodness' sake. I knew children, I had read everything that was recommended on natural birth and child raising, and after all, giving birth was something millions of women did every day. What was so scary about that!

I left at home to prepare. I completed my last assignment and planned to sit for my exam with my tutor to supervise me. I didn't have Mum close by to mind a baby, so I would have to take it with me. On my last doctor's visit, I was pronounced healthy, fit and ready. If the baby didn't come before the next appointment, my doctor would consider inducing.

I had packed my bag when there was a phone call from friends asking to come and visit on Saturday night.

'Come for dinner I offered', as the last time we had had dinner at their place. Friday, I launched into house cleaning, vacuuming, dusting and polishing furniture. I reasoned I had let housework slip while working on the last assignment, so it seemed natural to spruce the place up a bit. Friday night, back ache and slight nausea seemed a result of unexpected exertion. Saturday, I wasn't feeling myself, not ill exactly, just aching back, tired and restless, with funny niggly pains in my abdomen. I had heard the stories of the acute pain of delivery and didn't consider this constant niggle to be relevant. Our friends arrived, and I began to cook the meal, schnitzel with mushroom sauce. I started to feel really nauseous and told Val, a woman with three children, about my constant niggly pains and backache.

'Oh no', she said, 'you will know when labour really starts'.

Having served the meal, I excused myself and went to lie down. I couldn't have been there long when I had a sudden convulsion of pain and an immediate need to head to the bathroom. It was as if I vented the baby and all into the toilet. I sat there shaking, sobbing, not daring to look, when Val came in and said, 'That will have been your water breaking. We'd better get you to the hospital'.

When my husband ushered me into the maternity hospital, he was met with a stern 'No males allowed'.

I was actually grateful because now I realised I was out of my depth, and I really wanted professionals to look after me. Ushered into a darkened room, I was told, 'Just try to rest, dear. It could be a while'. Four hours later, I gave birth to a beautiful seven-pound boy. I had been three fingers dilated when I arrived, and my top-notch doctor just arrived in time.

In the days that followed, I was so attached to this tiny bundle of humanity that I couldn't leave him for an instant and decided not to bother sitting the important exam. I also decided to retire from teaching. The new career of motherhood seemed much more appealing.

Reg was absolutely besotted by the baby. At last, he had a son. The night of Michael's birth, he and several mates were heard in the local pub singing, 'Michael, row the boat ashore, hallelujah'.

There is no love quite like the love of a mother for her firstborn. It is all-consuming, surpassing the love for family, even partner. She is biologically primed for this. At the baby's cry, milk starts to seep from her breasts; when he doesn't cry, she feels a need to touch him to make sure he is still breathing. All her instincts are concentrated on keeping this baby safe, warm and loved. This was my entry into the world of motherhood.

The baby was my centre of attention. I fed him every time he cried and so stimulated copious amounts of milk. This led to him almost chocking on the delivery until the community nurse showed me how to feed him lying down, making him drink uphill to slow the rate. Lying down, suckling my baby, was absolute bliss.

CHAPTER 28

1968 – New Baby, New Home

WHEN MICHAEL WAS FOUR months old, we moved to Seaforth into a house owned by the Main Roads Department which we inherited from our friends. The house had been bought to demolish when the new freeway crossing Middle Harbour was built. That never happened, so we lived there for ten years. When Doug contacted the department to tell them he would be vacating in January, he gave them our details, including a reference from our landlord and an assurance that we would move in and do any necessary cleaning and repairs. I felt a little guilty at the number of people waiting for housing commission homes, but apparently, this is how it works with main roads. Doug won their house through a friend of a friend, and years later, we were able to acquire the house next door for our friends.

At this time, I felt I had found paradise. We were living in a two-bedroom house with a big backyard in a beautiful location, and I had a doting husband who idolised me and a perfect baby whom I idolised. I had nothing to do but play wife and mother, and three little girls visited every fortnight to play mother to a real live baby doll. Why did I not realise how lucky I was, and why did I jeopardise what I had?

Basically, I am very single-minded about what I want and very determined in achieving that, and what I wanted was a second baby. Reg didn't want another child; he was pushing forty and already had three daughters and the all-important son. He could not understand why I felt the need for more children. I was happy to wait a year, focusing my energies on the baby at home, but once Michael was walking and out of nappies, I was ready to launch into my new project. Simply by stopping the pill and letting nature take its course, I was pregnant fairly soon. However, that only lasted nearly four months, and a sudden gush of blood as I was cutting a birthday cake for the middle girl saw Reg driving me, three girls and a baby over the Harbour Bridge on a Saturday night to the same maternity hospital and doctor that I had had before, even though Manly Hospital would have been only ten minutes from home. The maternity staff assured me that my miscarriage was a good thing, nature's way of screening a foetus that shouldn't be born, and to go home to the baby you have.

Reg thought that might put an end to my desire and bought me a Labrador puppy instead. However, the experience only hardened my resolve. I was also worried that my abortion may have damaged my cervix, resulting in my never being able to carry another baby. After a couple of months, I was pregnant again, and Reg was not impressed. This time, I was very careful, no rushing, no stressing, no lifting the toddler. I even tried breathing and relaxation exercises. All to no avail. I had just felt the baby move inside me with a sudden gush of blood and dash to the hospital. This time, my doctor realised I was determined to have another baby, so he set out some rules to make it happen. He said, 'When you fall pregnant, I will stitch up your cervix so you will have to have a caesarean. Then you must observe a strict bed rest regime, morning and afternoon naps and early to bed, and absolutely no sex for the rest of the pregnancy'.

It was not a good practise to keep secrets from your partner, but I did not tell Reg about these rules until, pregnant again, I went to see the doctor, and as promised, he stitched my cervix. I feel the seed of our uncoupling was sown then.

Reg must have felt pushed out and ignored. He might have feared for me, wondering if I would miscarry while stitched up. Seven months seemed an eternity as I kept to my bed and willed the baby to stay. The caesarean was scheduled for Thursday morning, and I awoke late in the day to find no baby beside me. The nurse said, 'He will be in intensive care for two days, and no, you cannot see him'.

I was devastated, sure that he must be abnormal or near death's door. My husband had been told by my sister that he had a son, and as she said later, 'he didn't seem very interested'. That night, he came and had an altercation with the sister in charge as he was out of visiting hours and the ladies were feeding their babies, all except me that is, huddled under the blanket in tears as I hadn't seen, much less fed, my baby.

When Michael, now aged three, came with his dad to collect me, he was so thrilled with and possessive of the new baby, I knew I had done the right thing.

When it was time to renew marital relations because my stitch was still in place, it caused my husband discomfort. Now, as though secrecy between us had become the new norm, he didn't tell me, just avoided having sex. This naturally led to his turning to another woman.

'When a marriage is on the rocks, you can bet the rocks are in the bed'.

CHAPTER 29

1971 – Truth and Reconciliation

I NEED TO GO back a little and fill in necessary information about the time I spent obsessed with producing a second baby. My husband had great success with his new career as a sales representative for General Electric and scored a large bonus three years in a row for most successful salesperson. With this money, he bought a boat, a half cabin runabout, which he loved. He had always been keen to go to sea. At seventeen, he had joined the navy but really couldn't cope with military discipline. Once he had his own means to explore the waterways, he was in his element. I, on the other hand, had only just learned to swim and was not at all comfortable in or on the water.

Somehow Reg met two Dutch girls backpacking their way around the world, crewing on boats. They had come to Sydney to try to do the famous Sydney to Hobart race. A little runabout is hardly a contender for a sailing race, but Petra and Else were often venturing out with Reg into Sydney Harbour, where I refused to go, particularly with the babies. This was especially after we were hit by the bombora off Middle Head, where all three of us finished on the floor of the boat, fortunately not over the side.

This then was the precursor to my realization that there was now three in my marriage and that I did not want to stay in a relationship where love, on one side at least, seemed to have died. In the January holiday, I confronted Reg and assured him that I would facilitate his continuing relationship with the son he adored but that he would need to move out and leave me in the house. I assumed he would move in with the Dutch girls, but the very thought of becoming substitute parents to a nearly three-year-old scared these twenty-something girls that suddenly they were travelling north to try their luck on the Sunshine Coast.

My husband decided to stay with the family he had, and as a 'so sorry I ignored your needs' gesture, he booked me a two-hour trail ride at a riding school in Belrose while he minded the boys that Saturday. As luck would have it, the school was short-staffed that day, and I stayed four hours, helping take out rides. This, in turn, led to regular assisting, while my husband and our best friends, who were now our next-door neighbours, minded the children. So now I had my passion for horses fulfilled. Later that year, my husband even bought me a horse, saying,

'Could I have a look at this pony for sale as a customer of his wants to buy a pony for his child'.

That is how we came to acquire Charcoal, a beautiful, quiet grey, so trustworthy he would not move out of a slow jog unless the child had gained sufficient balance and, if the child fell off, he would stand still until they scrambled back on.

In July 1970, Karen, Reg's eldest daughter, turned fifteen and asked if she could invite some friends over to Seaforth and have a party on her actual birthday date. Now one would assume that I, being a high school teacher, for the last eight years, would know something about the perils of hosting a teenage birthday party, but I guess I was so elated with being five months pregnant, past the dangerous three-month stage where I had the miscarriages, and feeling healthy with not working, I was happy to agree. By now the girls were traveling to Seaforth by public transport, so that was what the additional four girls and four boys did, arriving about lunchtime. First problem, night-time accommodation, as we had insufficient beds. Not a problem, said Reg, the girls would sleep inside and the boys outside in the garage or we can pitch the tent. We had blow-up mattresses and sleeping bags for some, or they could bring their own. Next, transport to Clontarf Beach. Fortunately, Margaret, my friend and next-door neighbour, offered to come and use her Kombi van to take extra bodies. So about sunset, we set off to cook sausages and chops on the barbecue at Clontarf, with salads, a big birthday cake and cans of drink. What I didn't realise was that the boys had also brought along some drink of the alcoholic type, of which I was completely unaware. Reg was cooking the meat and Margaret was buttering bread when I noticed one of the boys was swinging on the door of the Kombi. I was enraged at his disrespect for the lady who had transported him and the obvious damage his actions may cause her car. I stormed over and told him to stop that nonsense and then unthinkingly blurted words I would instantly regret.

'If you want to act like a baboon, go climb a tree', which is exactly what he did, climbing a great gum to a great height and then falling with a thud to the ground.

This was in the days before mobile phones. We didn't know where the closest public phone would be and if it would be working. (So many of them were vandalised.) Reg decided to drive the boy, whose name I discovered was Neville, and a couple of friends to Manly Hospital, where he spent the night, having been diagnosed with a compact fracture of the arm. It was a very subdued party after that, but I still locked both doors to keep the sexes segregated. If a girl climbed out the window, that was her choice, not sanctioned by me.

By 1974, Reg had found another passion or rather rekindled an earlier quest. He had always loved live music. Before the children came along, we would frequent pubs playing live music and go to jazz festivals and all kinds of ethnic music. We already had a superb stereo system, but Reg wanted to improve the sound. He would be forever taking speaker boxes apart, changing components, re-padding, testing over and over again to find the purist sound. His best friend at this stage was Colin Waite, another sound perfectionist, and together, they worked towards improving recorded sound. Finally, they produced a prototype manufactured in our garage and perfected in our lounge room, and they entered it in the Sydney Hi-Fi Show held at the Boulevard Hotel. They decided to call their company AMW Speakers (Australia's Mahoney & Waite), and the reception was very positive. A reviewer praised it as being quite revolutionary and a worthwhile addition to any serious Hi-Fi enthusiast collection. Suddenly, we were getting orders. Members of the Sydney Symphony Orchestra were visiting to hear our speakers. International musicians were enquiring. Reg left GE, sold his boat, rented a workspace in

Cromer and hired two carpenters. The first order I heard and saw was a huge eight-stack set for the Daly-Wilson Big Band, who were playing at Narrabeen High School and whose lead singer was a very young Marcia Hynes. All the money went into building the business, so I put Greg into kindy and went back to work. Fortunately, the librarian at Narrabeen High School was taking a four-month-long service leave and considering retiring after that, so I had stable employment for the rest of the year.

Unfortunately, drugs are very much part of the music scene, and I would come home from work and smell the unmistakeable odour of marijuana. Orders were produced at the factory, but the constant evaluating and improving were taking place in our lounge room and increasingly under the delusional effect of smoking pot. My entreaties to consider the children fell on deaf ears.

'Send them next door' was the most frequent response. I considered moving out, especially after a student from Narrabeen High turned up one weekend and had the heavy pot smell all over him.

I had a ten-year-old Morris Minor that I needed to get to work. Unfortunately, when registration time came, it needed some work and new tyres, $300 dollars' worth all told. I didn't have any savings; the business was going bust, so I had to sell Charcoal to be able to drive my car. At first, I sold him to the riding school so I could keep an eye on him, but later, one of the mothers told me she really wanted to buy him for her child, so that was a very good option.

Colin's marriage was the first to break. He had been a suit-wearing accountant who had married an eccentric art student. As their relationship developed, Colin became more and more eccentric and pot smoking, and his wife, who was now working and paying the bills, became more and more conservative. Their divorce destroyed Colin and accentuated the financial decline of AMW. The final straw for me was when my husband, totally depressed by the failure of the business, attempted to take his own life, but before swallowing the tablets, he told his children he would not be there anymore. I called a friendly doctor, who did not report the attempt. That was the week before Christmas. On Christmas Eve, Reg did not come home, and the children, having emptied their Santa sacks, were anxious to open the presents under the tree. Fortunately, Karen, Reg's eldest daughter, arrived in time with his boyfriend Paul to be the guests for the opening of presents. When Reg arrived about lunchtime, he had enough flowers to fill a shop, all of them from a roadside stall, and boxes of chocolates for the boys. Boxing Day was always celebrated with our close friends. The atmosphere around Reg and I must have been somewhat strained, but no one said anything. The following day, Vicki, Reg's middle daughter, turned up on my doorstep just as I was about to visit a real estate agent. She was the one daughter I dreaded telling, but when I did, she said, 'About time too. I'll come and look at places with you'.

I hadn't realised how other people had seen the disintegration of my marriage.

So we found a two-bedroom flat in Balgowlah, on the bus route to Seaforth School, and the boys and I moved in New Year's Eve 1976. The next phase of my life as a single mum was about to begin.

CHAPTER 30

1977 — Life in a Duplex

IT WAS WITH VERY mixed feelings that I moved out of the Seaforth house. I had loved living there, looking out over a great expanse of open bushland, reserved for a freeway that would never be built. This was the house I had brought my babies to, expecting to stay until the bulldozers arrived. Now I didn't want to take anything away. I wanted the house to look the same when the boys came to visit their dad every second weekend. Consequently, and also because I couldn't afford a removalist van, all I took was the boys' double bunk cut into two single beds, their chest of drawers and their set of a toy table and two chairs, a folding chair for me, the mattress and doona from the spare bed, the picnic basket, the ironing board and iron and all our clothes. Interestingly, when I told the boys they could leave half their toys behind, they determinedly packed everything into the two cartons I provided. These, together with exactly half the towels, all the single sheets, half the pillow slips and tea towels and all the photo albums, were the entirety of my married life that I carried away. All fitted into the work ute of Paul, Reg's eldest daughter Karen's husband-to-be.

Leaving the dog and cat behind was my biggest heartbreak as pets were not allowed in the unit. A little under a week later, I came home to find Stumpy, our five-year-old fox terrier, tied up to the front gate, and he lived with us for the nine months we were there. Fortunately, the real estate agent was very sympathetic when I went to tell him the situation, and as long as there were no complaints from the other tenant or neighbours, Stumpy could stay. Once again, I was fortunate to have lovely neighbours who welcomed our dog.

All was not idyllic, however. Our duplex was right at the lights guarding Balgowlah Road on Condamine Street, so traffic noise was something we had to get used to. The boys grew sick of playing picnics at dinnertime, of not having a lounge and especially a television, so I went back home and recovered the TV and a couple of poufs, leaving a note to the effect that the boys needed this more than their dad did. Every time I needed something I had left behind, I was tempted to make another return and claim but resisted and gradually bought my own.

The effect of the separation on the boys was of constant concern to me. There was one lad living next door about the same age as my eldest, but in Seaforth, there had been a street full of children and a paddock opposite to run and play. Here they were confined, and although we took the dog walking every afternoon and joined Manly nippers on the weekend, I knew they felt restricted, not even a yard to throw a ball. That year, my seven-and-a-half-year-old wrote a story about a prince who had lost his palace and had to live in a dark dungeon.

Come the May holiday, I accepted an invitation from a girl I worked with, a single mother with two sons similar in age to mine, who suggested we three spend some time with her family living in a house in Avalon. I had never been that far up the peninsula before and fell in love with the village atmosphere of Avalon. After a week there, I was combing the real estate pages, looking somewhere cheap to buy.

CHAPTER 31

1978 — My First Home

THE FIRST HOUSE WAS on Pittwater Road and had no front yard as that had been resumed to widen the road. Inside was dark, cramped, stuffy and far too noisy.

The second was built like a concrete tomb, dark and intimidating, and had a peculiar mouldy smell like damp concrete. Too scary.

The third house was off the main road, up a small hill and halfway down a very leafy street. A stately gum tree in the front and the house itself seemed to smile a welcome with its two large open front windows. The entire front was clad to resemble a weatherboard and had a second smaller closed window. An extended roof formed a car port, sheltering the side door, and a hotchpotch of colourful plants lined the low fence. First impressions: just right.

We entered the front room, which seemed cool on this hot January day, and everything smelt new and fresh. The front room had a lovely polished wooden floor and a timbre feature wall with a servery showing a small but adequate kitchen. Through the front windows, you could see not only the beautiful gum tree but also a lovely collection of flowering bottlebrushes from the house across the road.

The real estate agent explained that this house had been a deceased estate, a single-bedroom property, owned by an elderly lady. An enterprising young builder had bought it and added this new room to make the house seven squares, just enough for the next buyer to be able to get a mortgage.

So the second closed window was the only bedroom, and this room revealed the house's age. Pre-gyprock plaster ceiling and walls complete with picture rail. There was an ancient wooden wardrobe and the carpet, I'm sure, was older than me. Inside, the room smelt of age and eau de cologne (or maybe that was the carpet cleaner). I was struck with the very old and the very new next to each other. Through a reasonable dining room, also with picture rail and carpet smelling its age, and into a tiny kitchen, clean and adequate, even if the electric stove had seen many hard years' toil. Then to the bathroom, backing onto the kitchen. A deep bath with overhead shower and an old-fashioned gas heater, the type that had once singed my eyelashes and eyebrow. It would be the first thing to go.

Where was the toilet? Outside. Sewerage hadn't reached Avalon at that stage, and this was a relic of the dunny cart days, and it still smelt that way. Actually, it was a pump-out septic tank. That was a new problem I was to learn about in the future.

As I gazed at the huge backyard, with only one fence on the left-hand side, I saw the clothes line, a cord strung between two posts, with a clothes prop to hold it up, and shaded by a magnificent mulberry tree (now there is a minefield for clean white sheets). I looked up at the hill to Whale Beach, and I knew that heavy rain would probably rush down there and flood this block, but I had fallen in love with this little oddity of a house. The boys could have the bedroom, and I would sleep in the lounge, and the dining room was big enough to house a wardrobe for me. Living problems solved. Now for the financial, I desperately wanted to buy this house.

And with a little help from the bank, I did.

Haiku: Lovely house so cool, proudly old but brightly new, please be my haven.

CHAPTER 32

Living in Avalon

BOTH BOYS WERE HAPPY to move into my new home as a house walking distance from the beach was an exciting prospect. Fortunately, we moved in the September school holiday, which meant the boys would only be newcomers for one term. In 1979, they would return as regular Avalon boys. Football had finished, nippers was due to start, and both boys were anxious to join. In many ways, they found it easier to fit in to this new society than I did. Both had been reasonably popular at Seaforth School, having a large number of friends, both boys and girls. By the end of the first week of holidays, they had made friends with a boy just three doors down, one year younger than Michael and with an older sister who just loved horses. This was to prove very useful to me in the coming weeks as I could leave my sport-mad son with her brother and take her to spend the day with horses. I remember taking my boys to school on day 1 and confiding to the principal that I had recently left their father and was hoping that maybe they could be in a class with a male teacher for necessary male bonding. The principal sighed and told me at least one third of the entire school population was in the same predicament, and he only had two male staff members, neither of whom were available for my boys. So different from the Seaforth School population, with the clear majority of students having two parents at home. I was to discover this had led to my not being as accepted by the other mums, as if being an unattached female was a threat to their stability.

I think it is time I filled in some details about my boys. Michael, the eldest, the longed-for son and heir, was a very determined and imaginative child. From the very beginning, where he sucked so hard at the breast and became so winded and bloated that he had to nurse drinking uphill, everything he did, he did with gusto. When playing with a favourite toy truck, he would fill the tip body to overflowing and be so determined to make everything fit, keeping things in until they no longer fell out. This resulted in him starring in a commercial. Our next-door neighbour in Seaforth was a freelance photographer, and one day, he chatted to me as I gardened and Michael played at filling his truck. He said he had a project to make an advertisement for a new rear-view mirror for a truck, and the following day, he came with a delivery van and parked it in our drive. Our front lawn had a steep incline towards the street, and the idea was for Michael and his truck to be at the top near the steps, and then, while the delivery man walked his parcel up the stairs, I was to bump the truck so that it rolled towards the drive and would hit the concrete path and spill its contents. Michael would hopefully crawl down, sit and put everything back into the truck. The photographer spent some time working on the right trajectory the truck would take and marked out where everyone had to be, van, Michael and Ie. That afternoon, he made the clip. The delivery man arrived, walked up the stairs and rang the doorbell. I bumped the truck, and off it trundled down the grassy slope, hit the path and spilled its contents. Immediately, Michael set off at a rapid crawl, found his truck and proceeded to fill it. The delivery man came back, climbed into his van and started the engine. That caused Michael to look up, and the driver opened the rear-view mirror in the floor. There was this beautiful picture of a slightly bemused toddler sitting right where he would have been run over had the van moved!

That advertisement travelled the country at truck and country shows. I was given $50, with which I opened a bank account for Michael.

Once Michael started walking, he loved to dance. If any music played, he would move to the rhythm. I took a photo of him in front of the television dancing to Sue Becker's *Jazzercize* programme. At about age five, I took him and the girls to see *Swan Lake* the ballet. Michael was so enthralled when the hero defeated the villain, he spontaneously stood up and cheered. At about the same age, we four went to see a *Music for Children* at the Opera House, and Michael was so eager to perform, he was chosen to go on stage and be Pamino, the heroine, sitting on a ladder as Papageno sang to her. Because he had a head full of golden curls, the compere didn't realise he had chosen a boy to be the lady.

The usual fantasy heroes were important, and Michael would work the bar swing up to its full steam and leap into the air like Superman. Reg had taken a photo of him in a Superman T-shirt, blue swimmers and red cape, with arms outstretched, leaping off the swing. Taken from below, it showed Michael reaching out, passing the house roof, so he was convinced that one day he had actually flown. Unfortunately, he kept trying to repeat that performance and pushing the swing to its upmost that one day he leapt off and broke his arm.

Michael's most memorable lapse into fantasy was on a caravan holiday in 1975 when we camped near a fast-flowing river outside Oberon. Suddenly, Michael was no longer in sight! The girls, Reg and I ran along the riverbank, calling Michael, with no response. Then Reg rushed to the car, saying, 'You stay here if he reappears. I am going to get help'. At the sound of the car driving away, suddenly, Michael appeared from the bushes.

He was being Robin Hood, and the evil sheriff's men were after him!

Unfortunately, he did not completely lose that need for make-believe in his life. On his eleventh birthday, I had five eleven-year-old boys in the car looking for places to ride a skateboard. One of them had an accident and cut his toe, requiring stitches. I was at Mona Vale hospital and didn't realise the nurse was calling my name as she was calling Mrs Mooney. Then one of the boys told me Michael's father was Tom Mooney, a Sea Eagles player!

Gregory, the second child, didn't need an imaginative world; he had his big brother and next-door neighbour as playmates, and his whole life seemed to revolve around keeping up with them. His nickname was 'me too' as he said it so often. He seemed to lack a sense of caution, believing he could do anything the bigger boys did. Once while playing chasings, he rode his toy horse down a flight of seven steps, crashed and split his lip, requiring stitches. He was riding the horse because he said it went faster than he could run and helped him keep up. It is strange that Greg, the baby Reg didn't want, became his dad's favourite and would spend weekends in Seaforth, while Michael, the chosen one, refused to miss his sporting commitments. I realised we were not Michael's preferred choice of parents. In his last year with the Harbord Swimming Club, the point score revealed Michael had tied for first place. He was not the champion swimmer, just the child who never missed a meeting and swam in every event. He had our next-door neighbour Peter Deville to thank for this. He religiously took his lad and both of mine to freshwater pool every Saturday.

Apart from endeavouring to keep up with boys three and four years older, Greg's secret defence was he could fall asleep anywhere, anytime. Quite often, Michael would come in to say, 'We can't find Greg'. At first, this caused minor panic, but after discovering him asleep in a cupboard, under a bed and behind bushes in the garden, we realised a very small boy needs to rest when he is expending so much energy, so we would go looking for his latest hideaway.

In November 1978, Karen married Paul, and of course, Reg's parents came to the wedding and stayed in the house in Seaforth. I was quite embarrassed to find Nell, Reg's mother, carefully setting the coffee table for tea using two large doilies as place mats. I had taken the dining room table when Sharon and her son moved in, and they used the dining room as a bedroom. I was even more embarrassed when Reg's mum wanted to iron Reg's shirt as I had taken the ironing board and iron, justifying that Reg didn't use them. The following year, Karen and Paul bought a lovely little one-bedroom house in Clareville, an adjoining suburb of Avalon. In the following years, they transformed that house into a two-storey, four-bedroom palace as their children Jesse, Matt and Alicia were born.

CHAPTER 33

The BMX Project and a Chance Encounter

IN 1979, MICHAEL'S LAST year and Greg's first year at Avalon Primary School, a significant event took place. A staff member had recently returned from spending time at an orphanage in Cambodia and was filled with zeal to raise money to build a school building. A local business had donated a BMX bike as a prize, and the primary school children were encouraged to sell tickets to buy bricks to build the school. Michael and Greg hatched a plan to join forces to win the bike. They would canvas the Seaforth area when they visited Reg, the riding school when they came with me and the Avalon area as well. Michael told me he wanted Greg to have the bike as he really didn't want a BMX, and if they did win, he asked if Reg and I could buy him a racing bike instead. I didn't really think they had much chance of winning as some parts of Avalon, Whale Beach and Palm Beach are quite wealthy, and I thought those parents would subsidise their children's efforts, so I agreed. I had underestimated my son's dogged persistence.

Greg literally cleaned up in Seaforth. The parents were so impressed by his heartfelt story of poor orphans who didn't have a school and how he was helping his teacher raise money to build one that $5 and $10 donations were not infrequent. Riding school patrons were likewise generous. However, the most generous donation of all came from a house in Whale Beach the boys visited one Sunday. A group of four couples were having lunch and, upon hearing the story, decided to contribute $100! Michael told me excitedly that I had been invited to lunch the following Sunday to meet these lovely people. I couldn't make lunch but agreed to go for coffee after I finished at the riding school, and that was how the boys and I met the infamous paedophile, Phillip Bell.

Some two weeks later, I went to Whale Beach and met Phillip; a couple from Manly with their son, Mathew; a Dutch couple from Mona Vale with their daughter, Gaby, and son, Arn; Philip's secretary, Barbara; and a couple of other surfing mates of the children. The children were all much older than mine, having left school, and the parents were entranced with my little ones, being so committed to such a noble cause.

Philip told me that he always wanted to meet the parents of the children who dropped in to his place and that he always had the children's best interests at heart. He emphasised on good manners, did not encourage drinking other than a glass of wine with meals, banned cigarettes and frowned on swearing in front of ladies or children. Drugs were definitely a no-go area. This was music to my ears, and I was happy to allow Michael to drop in to Phillip's home after surfing at Whale Beach. It wasn't until Michael went to Barrenjoey High that he heard from other pupils about 'Pedo Phil', but by that time, he had formed a friendship and could see nothing wrong with the man. The other boys agreed that Phil was harmless; they just made fun of him behind his back, but Michael defended his friend, and as he told me, 'Phillip is like a father to me. He talks about what I need to do to get on in the world and maybe become a financier like him'.

I talked to Karen's boyfriend, Paul, about what should I do about this friendship, and he said, 'Michael would let you know if he starts any funny stuff, and at present, it looks as if his influence is all good'.

Reg also went to visit Phillip and was quick to lay it on the line if Phillip laid a finger on Michael, he would tear him apart. Phillip bought a set of AMW speakers and lent Reg a car so he could take both boys to see their paternal grandparents, who were living in Batemans Bay at the time.

Why did I not tell Michael to have nothing to do with Phillip Bell? Firstly, I think Michael would not have listened to me. He was impressed with the man who explained things like stocks and shares and how to make money, something both his parents seemed to be uninterested in. Phillip shared his love of surfing, unlike his parents, and he seemed so sophisticated, well read, well-travelled and interested in Michael's dreams and aspirations.

Then there was my reliance on my gut instinct in judging people. I genuinely believed that Phillip would never harm my boy, that he had his best interests at heart and that he was a shining example of drug-free, non-smoking, alcohol in moderation, supporter of education, that I needed to influence my sons. There was also my avoidance of using a label to describe anyone, be it aborigine, Asian, homosexual, Muslim or refugee. You judge people by what they do and say, not what they may be.

So 1979 was quite a momentous year. Michael and Greg's efforts won them the BMX bike, which became Greg's. Phillip gave me $50 towards Michael's racing bike.

That year, Michael sang in the combined primary school children's choir at the Sydney Opera House. His teacher, a very forthright lady and deputy principal, also ran the school choir and insisted that her entire class be founding members. Gradually, many dropped out, but many found joy in singing and stayed on, boys in particular who would never have joined of their own accord. I had tears in my eyes as I sat in the audience and watched them singing their hearts out with a full orchestra and the magnificent organ accompanying them. Memories of my magical time at Sydney Town Hall came flooding back, and I felt so grateful to the education system that offers such a wonderful experience to any child who participates.

Michael's surfing at Whale Beach and dropping in to Phillip's place for a snack afterwards continued, and so did Phillip's influence over him. As Phillip told me, Michael was the first of his surfing boys to actually want to use his brain to get ahead in the world, and he wanted to encourage this. Consequently, in second year, Michael selected French and commerce as his elective subjects, and this led to a night at the Opera for Michael and I with Phillip to see Don Giovani sung in French. Once again, Michael was totally wrapped in the performance, amazed that he could interpret some of the language and very happy with the English storyline given in the prompt board above the stage.

Phillip was totally thrilled with his protégé's progression in his studies and cultural development and started to talk to me about his plans for schooling overseas to really put the polish on Michael's performance. He told me he had been sent to school in Switzerland in his teens to be immersed in the French and German languages which stood him in such good stead in his financial career. At first, this seemed unbelievable, but once winter came, Karen and Paul were going to the snowfields, and the boys so wanted to experience snow, so I hired a station wagon and drove to Jindabyne, we three sleeping in the back and venturing out to play in the snow. Both boys were hooked on the possibilities of skiing.

Phillip's plan was to take Michael out of term 3 in year 8 and enrol him in the international school in Geneva. He would board with an English couple, Sue and Patrick Paget, who were long-term friends of Phillip and who had two sons, one older and one younger than Michael. Phillip said he had promised those two boys a Sydney surfing holiday with him, and the older boy had already stayed for a month with the Manly couple, and soon it would be the younger one's turn, and he could stay with me. The whole deal would be like a school exchange programme. Michael was so excited by the prospect, and it seemed such a wonderful idea. I had correspondence back and forth with Sue Paget, and she thought it was a wonderful idea too, so I went ahead and organised a passport for Michael. Reg was not keen, but faced with Michael's enthusiasm and excitement, he agreed. Phillip was going to take another business trip to Geneva to settle Michael into his new home. It was with mixed feelings that I farewelled them both at Sydney International Airport. I was losing my baby boy; he would return with more worldly experience, more linguistic skill and who knows what new attitudes and beliefs. But I was firm in the belief this was an unmissable opportunity to grow and excel, which would put him at an advantage in the desperate climb up the corporate ladder. A destiny he had chosen for himself from the age of six, where unbeknown to me, he had put his toys for sale in the Sunday paper's Charlie Chuckles Kid's page.

I decided weekly phone calls were essential and planned to pay my phone bill via credit card to make this possible. There was also the monthly letter, which we had promised each other. News was excellent. He loved the Pagets, was mates with the sons and was finding schoolwork okay. Math was harder, his French wasn't as good as he had thought, but English was great as he had already done Shakespeare's *Julius Caesar*. As a special treat, the Pagets had taken the three boys on a horse-riding day out, knowing that this was something Michael was good at, whereas winter sports were something new.

Phillip wrote to me from London with his next proposal. He felt Michael had adjusted well to European schooling and was progressing well academically. He felt the next step should be boarding school, a total immersion in foreign languages and a prestigious mention on his CV. The school Phillip wanted to send Michael to was in Gstaad, Switzerland, the one he had attended. I could understand Phillip wanting to send Michael there and be willing to pay for it. Phillip looked upon his boys as the sons he couldn't have and wanted to do things a father would do. I had already accompanied Phillip to the wedding of Chippy, one of the older surfer boys, and knew Phillip had put a deposit down on a property for him. So I could understand Phillip's motivation, but what about Michael and boarding school? Well, of course, this school was in the Swiss mountains, so skiing would be the chosen sport. Michael was so excited to go there. To ally my fears about Michael's readiness for boarding school, Phillip suggested I spend Christmas with him in Switzerland, and he sent me an airline ticket to make this possible.

CHAPTER 34

1981 - My Trip to Europe

LATE SEPTEMBER 1981 AND I just received an Air India ticket to Paris with open travel dates to be used by March 1982. However, I didn't have a passport, so off I went to apply for an Australian passport, complete with birth certificate, record of adoption, marriage certificate and driver's licence. Of course, what I didn't have was a certificate of Australian citizenship. I hadn't had the need for it before and didn't bother when my mother and stepfather became citizens some years back.

Okay, so how do I become an Australian citizen? Which form do I have to fill in? I am so sure that I have all the qualifications to be an Australian citizen. I have lived here since I was six years old. I have married an Australian, borne two Australian sons and worked for the New South Wales government for two decades, and I really do feel Australian; this is my home!

Apparently, my qualifications were not good enough to get citizenship this year. I had to wait until 26 January 1982 to present at an Australian citizenship ceremony to become an Australian. Suddenly, I felt very, very British. Could I get a British passport before Christmas? I had to pay an exorbitant amount of money, but yes, I got my British passport on 27 November. So now I thought I was set to go. Reg was taking Greg to spend Xmas with his parents this year, so he was organised. I told Greg that I would save up to take him overseas next year before he turned twelve so he would travel for half price.

Fortunately, I told Pam from the riding school about needing to get a British passport because she advised me I would need a re-entry visa to get back into Australia. Years later, I read about a young English man who had come to Australia as a young child, had married an Australian girl and decided to honeymoon in Fiji. When they tried to return to Australia, his wife, with an Australian passport, could board, but with an English passport and no re-entry visa, he was not allowed and had to extend his stay in Fiji to sort out a return visa. Fortunately, I was able to get mine on 17 December! Unfortunately, I didn't have further conversation with Pam about not having a confirmed return flight booking. I had been told my ticket could be used from five different cities: London, Paris, Frankfurt, Athens and Rome. I was wait-listed from all of these, back to Australia at the end of January, but of course, this is the most popular time for Australians to return. What I didn't realise was that I was waiting for a cancelation that would not be snapped up by someone paying a premium fare. I was so naïve and unworldly in the world of transport. Today, I wouldn't dream of boarding a flight without a confirmed return booking. Back then, the fact that I was actually going to Europe was all a bit unbelievable, so I floated along in a dream.

My flight out of Australia was scheduled for 29 December, so it was a lonely Xmas day for me as Reg and Greg had left to spend Xmas in Batemans Bay. I had used my new credit card to complete my Xmas shopping for the Paget family, all small trinkets to pack easily. As it would be winter in Europe, I packed skivvies, tights and jumpers, not realizing how heated everything is indoors. My first purchase in Switzerland was a cotton shirt! I had scoured the municipal library for books on Switzerland, Paris and Rome as I hoped to spend the four weeks I had visiting these places. I had photocopied relevant parts of *Let's Go Europe* and was ready to see the world!

After a long, tiring flight, Phillip met me at the Beauvais Airport in Paris on New Year's Eve, and we drove to a little town called Yvoire to welcome in the New Year. Later, I was to learn that this town was considered to be one of the loveliest villages in France. Such a culture shock for me. The brisk winter chill, the stark leafless trees, the medieval stone buildings, and a lovely, warm café with a delicious aroma of home-cooked meals. Seeing French families with copious carafes of wine, for children as well, the noise and the laughter, I really felt I was in a new fantasy world. Then the fireworks, chiming bells, everyone Bon Noel and kissing everyone else, including me. Not a single drunk or disorderly person in sight, just wonderful happiness and love.

We stayed the night and drove to Geneva the following day to meet the Paget family and Michael. What an emotional greeting, and how he had changed. Taller, slimmer, but still very confident and positive about his future plans. This included boarding school as being just the thing as long as he could be back in Australia to do the HSC.

Susan Paget confided to me that the boarding school Phillip proposed was considered to be one of the best in Europe and she would have loved to send her boys there but just could not afford it, so I was so lucky that my son had this opportunity. The following day, Michael had a surprise for me. Fortunately, I was wearing jeans and solid shoes as we went to the riding school where the Pagets had taken Michael and they had booked an indoor lesson for both of us as a late Xmas present. So paltry did my trinkets seem then, and what a wonderful present that was. An hour riding with my son, including jumping!

Then we were off to Gstaad to enrol Michael.

The main campus of Le Rosey Boarding School was in Rolle, a town forty kilometres to the north of Geneva and on the lake, but in January, the entire school moved to the Gstaat campus, 150 kilometres from Geneva, in the alps, where skiing was the main sport. Phillip, Michael and I drove to the village of Gstaat and stayed in a lovely country house, where Phillip rented the flat upstairs when he came to ski. The flat had two bedrooms, one with double bed and one with twin beds, that Michael and I shared. There had not been a great amount of snow, so we were able to walk down to the township, past the little stone church with the doorway open and neatly kept graves and headstones, to the main café where we had a delicious meal.

The following day, we drove up to the main Rosey campus, a series of alpine lodges, looking out over a spectacular view. There were students of all nationalities mingling in the enormous hall. Sound of various languages provided a cacophonous noise, and when the headmaster stood and greeted us, he did so in three languages, French, English and German. He said that the motto of the school was 'Learning for life' and that Le Rosy aimed to give students a comprehensive coverage of all the most important aspects of life, not only academia, but also music, art, sport and especially an understanding of different cultures, religions and beliefs, to encourage compassion and the ability to live harmoniously in peace. I was inspired, and Michael hugged me and said, 'I am really going to do my best here and make you proud'.

Back in Geneva, Phillip was to return to Australia and me to start my European backpacking adventure. I still did not have a fully confirmed ticket home. Sue Paget had offered to help me and obtained a confirmed ticket on 28 January from Paris to Bombay, wait-listed to Sydney. As that was the best offer I could get at that time, I decided to accept it. Well, I had a ticket. I would just have to wait on the wait list until I was confirmed, and India should surely be a cheap country to stay.

Just before I set off, I had a magical night in Geneva. The Pagets had a season subscription to the ballet, and the night before I was due to leave was the opening performance. Sue's husband offered me his ticket, saying I would probably enjoy ballet more than he would, and I was so excited to go. I did feel a little like Cinderella, not having the right clothes to go to a special event. I did have the basic black pants and black top, but my shabby duffel coat did not look respectable, and Sue was a very petite lady, so her jackets wouldn't fit me. So, inspired by Sue, we went shopping and found a wonderful fake fur coat that made me feel like a film star. It was the first extravagant purchase on my new credit card, but I felt it was so worth it. Now I could say I had seen opera in the Sydney Opera House and ballet in the Grand Theatre De Geneva!

I had expected my return flight would be from Paris, and I knew I would have nearly three weeks travelling, so I decided to see Italy first, stopping in Milan, Venice, Florence and Rome, allowing three days' stay and one day travelling in each. Again, with Sue's help, I had purchased a Travel Europe by Train Card so my travel expenses were covered, and I had *Let's Go Europe* recommendations for cheap lodgings calculated and felt I could eat sparingly and so make the most of this opportunity. The credit card was my security and fallback position if I needed to splurge.

CHAPTER 35

My Backpacking Adventure Begins — Italy

AS THE TRAIN EMERGED from a long tunnel, the change from the green Swiss countryside to the pink stone of Italy was dramatic. I didn't need a sign to tell me I was in Italy; I just knew, from the rocky countryside and houses painted pink and blue, I was in a different country. The guard checking my passport proved this.

The train to Milan took nearly eight hours, but at least I arrived in daylight and, with photocopied map in hand, proceeded to find a bed for the night. Suddenly, I was faced with a real problem. It was winter. Milan was not a tourist city, so backpacker hostels were closed! Why had I missed this important piece of information? As I trudged unfamiliar streets, finding closed signs, I wondered whether I had to splurge on a real hotel or catch the next train to Venice, maybe arriving in the dark, or wait till morning at the station. Obviously, I was not the first uninitiated traveller to find myself in this position, as I sat on a bench near the famous Milan Opera House, a well-dressed middle-aged man approached me and asked in heavily accented English if I needed accommodation. I replied I did but could not afford the nearby Square Hotel.

'My friend has a pensione not far from here that will cost you minimum lire per night. Would you like to follow me?'

Feeling as if I had little option, I walked with him some distance, which I tried to follow on my map, when we came to a very shabby two-storey building with an eatery of sorts on the ground floor. My companion conversed with the woman in charge and told me that for 100 lire, I could have a bed for the night and a meal, so I agreed. Upstairs was a long corridor with numerous doors, all using the one toilet and washbasin at one end. Inside the room was one antiquated double bed, a table and chair and a single light hanging from the ceiling. The meal consisted of a bowl of pasta with a strange sauce; the wine or water cost extra. My first real night as a backpacker was not what I expected, and I wondered what was in store!

The next morning, the lady showed me the route to the train station on my map, and I was able to catch the next train to Venice.

From Milan to Venice by train took a little over three hours, but when I arrived at Venezia Mestre station, this was not the Venice I had seen in travel brochures, but a rather dirty railway town, no sign of the water anywhere! It turned out that I had left the train at the terminal on the mainland and had to catch another train to cross the lagoon to Santa Lucia station on the island of Venice. Those trains were quite frequent, but I still cursed myself for not reading the Venice section carefully and only bringing a photocopied map of the island and addresses of possible accommodation. Even though I had a map and address, finding my way to the accommodation was quite tricky as I knew no Italian and met no one who spoke English. Finally, at the second address in the Cannaregio district, I had luck; a room was available for three nights, so I was able to drop my bag and set out to explore.

I am sure everyone who travels to Venice without a tour guide will get lost. The area is basically flat, so there is no high point to find a landmark to head to. The streets are narrow and windy, no cars, but myriads of small squares filled with mainly male locals sitting, invariably smoking, engaged in noisy conversation and sudden laughter. I was constantly reminded of Shakespeare's play *The Merchant of Venice*. Occasionally, I would approach a smallish group and, inspired by my feelings of having walked into a stage setting, would mime my predicament: being lost and wanting to find the water, boats and big church. Eventually, I found St Mark's Square, and even though it was winter, tourists were there in hordes. I was pleased I had been lost in Venice, wandering the quiet streets, trying to communicate without any common language, but a lot of laughter. I did meet a young English couple who had visited the Youth Hostel on another island of Venice and found it to be closed, so I was so happy to have found lodgings. The pair advised me to take the main vaporetto from Pier One and travel to Lido and back to get a good look at the Grand Canal. This I did, and what a wonderful trip it was.

Back to Piazza San Marco and the magnificent domed cathedral, simply breathtaking. I had been so busy planning where I would go and stay, I hadn't given too much thought as to what I would see and just felt totally overwhelmed by the experience. I promised myself I would read about everything when I returned home, and now my experience would be through my eyes and emotions. So much detail to absorb, so many statues, carving, mosaics, would my brain be able to maintain a complete memory? At that moment, I knew I would never return to Venice, so I had to make this visit worthwhile. Upon entering, I was engulfed by the sheer size of St Marks. St Mary's Cathedral in Sydney was my benchmark for cathedrals, and it would have been swallowed ten times over. Looking up into the domes, decorated by mosaic biblical scenes, made me dizzy and awe inspired. I had to sit at a pew and just breathe in the holy atmosphere.

Next door was the Palazzo Ducale, home of Venice's rulers for centuries. If I hadn't noticed before, pink was the preferred colour for homes in Italy, but of course, this was pink marble with a wondrous soft glow. This time, I had to be content with just the beautiful outside as there was a charge to visit. Thank goodness churches are traditionally open to all. Then it was time to make my way back to my lodging, made easier by a printed card the landlord had given me.

My second day was spent visiting the Bridge of Sighs and looking at markets with so many copies of Italian masterpieces, beautiful blown glass pieces and magnificent masks, costumes, and fabulous fabrics ready for carnival later in the year. My only purchase was essential food and water.

On to Florence, three hours by train. Arriving at Stazione Centrale di Santa Maria Novella, I was pleased to see the orange dome of Florence Cathedral. There was a high point one could surely see from anywhere in the town, and my address had been advertised as in the shadow of the Duomo. According to my photocopied map, this was quite close, so I hurried there, hoping Florence did not shut for the winter. Fortunately, Florence was a student town, so many art students flocked to Florence to study art in the many galleries. Unfortunately, I was a philistine in the art world and didn't bother to go and see the many European masterpieces on display, telling myself that as a school librarian with an extensive art collection back home, I could see and read about the great works I was missing later. Years later, on a trip to Provence, I realised what a marvellous experience it is to see real art masterpieces. Then in 2020, I was amazed by the sound and light show 'Van Gogh' and the following year, 'Renoir and Friends'. How wonderful that these shows came to Australia and how fortunate was I to be able to see them. Back to Florence in 1982, I was lucky to stumble across a copy of the memorable statue David by Michelangelo, which stood in Piazza della Signoria. I did recognise the work but didn't realise it was only a copy, the original being locked away in the art gallery. However, I did frequent churches, which were freely open, so I was exposed to much religious art and sculpture.

Finally, I made a spending splurge when I went to visit the church Santa Croce. In one of the little streets surrounding the church, there were several shoe shops. One had the most beautiful pair of boots I had ever seen. They were black leather, medium heel with a slash of red velvet inserted in the sides, just stunning. As I gazed at them, I thought of the outfit I had worn to the ballet in Geneva and how these boots would have perfectly suited the plain black outfit with the fake fur coat. Suddenly, the credit card was in my hand, and the deal was done. I loved those boots but seldom wore them and literally cried when a new puppy in the house chewed one irreparably.

Swearing that would be the only expensive amount to be credited this trip, I took the train to Rome. The four hours it took would have been through the beautiful Tuscan countryside, which I have read and seen in movies in later years, but my actual recollection of seeing it is very vague. I guess I was a typical first-time-in-Europe tourist, hungry to see the big attractions, with little interest in the actual country I was traveling through. Much later, I would think, if only I could have that time again, how I would savour every little experience. I did determine never to do the broad European trip but to take one country at a time and try to really become absorbed in every aspect. All of that was to be some time in the future when I became more affluent.

Arriving at the Central Rome terminal, I consulted my list of accommodations. Luckily, most cheap places were fairly close to the station, so I set off following my photocopied map. Rome is a tourist town, and places were open, but it took three addresses before I found a vacant dormitory hostel. It was now late afternoon, but still early enough to wander local streets and get my bearings. The first sudden change for me was the amount of traffic and the speed at which it travelled. I was literally terrified to cross the road until I found street lights. This meant that I travelled farther from the place of my lodging than usual but kept to the main streets on my map to be able to find my way back. The shadows were lengthening, so I thought of heading back when suddenly, there was a huge opening and what must surely be the Colosseum right in front of me. Lights were already illuminating the interior, and its sheer size and splendour absolutely overwhelmed me that I had to sit down. The light proved to be inadequate to take a photo, and just trying to fit proportions into the viewfinder seemed impossible, so I just breathed in the magnificence and vowed the experience was worth more than a photo. It surprised me how moved I was by the spectacle. It was not as if I hadn't seen really good photographs and movie representations of the building; I loved teaching ancient Rome. I wasn't even inside the parameters where tourists can go, but to stumble upon it, particularly at night-time, gave me an experience I would never forget.

The following morning, over breakfast, I met two English girls who were going to see the Vatican and asked me if I wanted to join them. They were carrying a complete travel guide and had worked out that the metro was the closest means of transport, so I followed them. Their travel guide suggested alighting at Stazione di San Pietro, the stop before the Vatican, and walking to the main entrance of Piazza San Pietro. Obviously, so many tourists followed this route that the entire street was filled with little shops selling religious statues and paintings. The walk to the Vatican was quite an experience in itself, particularly as every shop seemed to be filled with vocal Italians seemingly overcome by one or another purchase.

Piazza San Pietro was a huge circular walled plaza in front of the cathedral, where the pope would bless the multitudes who gather there on Sundays and religious occasions. This day, several groups of nuns were hurrying towards the steps, so we followed them. Thankfully, in accordance with Catholic principles, there was no charge to enter St Peters, although there was a charge to visit the Vatican Museums and the Sistine Chapel. Fortunately for me, the Sistine Chapel was closed for renovations, a common occurrence during winter months, so I was not embarrassed by having to decide whether I could afford to visit the most spectacular site in Christendom. Looking back, I cringe at the thought I could spend money on a pair of boots but be reluctant to pay for what would have been an amazing experience. Then again, without meeting the English girls, I may have forgone the trip to the Vatican altogether; it wasn't part of my photocopied sheets! Once again, I was struck by the sheer size and majesty of the building. This was surely the most impressive cathedral I had ever seen, surpassing even St Marks of Venice. Two significant experiences I can still recall today were climbing the very narrow winding steps up into the dome and gazing out from the top very briefly as feelings of nausea threatened to overcome me and then seeing Michelangelo's statue Pietà safely tucked behind a glass wall after being attacked some years back.

Once again, I was literally weak at the knees and holding my breath with awe at this sight. The marble was almost translucent, like living, breathing skin, except that the Christ figure was obviously dead and Mary was very much alive. His relaxed form, his arms and legs without that essence of life, compared to her beautifully crafted figure, so alive. Her face pictured deep love, deep sadness, overwhelming pity and total peace and acceptance. I remembered having seen a picture of this work and thinking no picture can compare with seeing the real thing.

I left St Peters feeling like a born-again Christian; I had been so touched by beauty and art.

The girls were going to visit the Spanish Steps and the Trevi Fountain as both were accessible by metro, so once again, I followed them. Thinking about it later, I decided that had not been the smartest decision. From the metro station to the Spanish Steps was just a sea of tourists, which continued down to the Keats-Shelley House. Well, what did I expect? This area had to be the most visited site by non-religious tourists, which had been me, but in my new semi-religious state, I was totally repulsed by the crowd. At least we found square slabs of pizza, something I hadn't seen before, for lunch. We continued our walk to the Trevi Fountain, and once again, I was annoyed by streams of tourists throwing coins into the fountain and angling to get the best photo of the site. Of course, the statues in the fountain, as magnificent as they were, could not compare to Michelangelo's Pietà, so I was not impressed, although I did like the two horses pulling the chariot, one sedate and one quite wild. The girls wanted to return that evening to see the fountain lit up, but I declined as I had seen enough. The following day, I wanted to visit the real ancient Rome.

Next morning, I walked to the Colosseum again as I had been told the ancient centre of Rome was immediately behind that building. Seeing it in daylight was like revisiting an old friend who was now showing its age. Still huge, but definitely broken and ancient. I found my way to the entrance and paid for a ticket which included entrance to the Colosseum. I certainly wished I had a complete travel guide with me as the entire forum was a city in itself, with a broad walkway, where I could imagine battalions of soldiers would have marched, bringing trophies home to Rome. Enormous marble pillars marking the entrance to temples, massive brick buildings side by side, statues in rows, and the whole area carpeted with green grass and clumpy bushes. There were tourists aplenty, but mainly in neat tour group packs or single or double individuals, all behaving in keeping with the solemnity of the site. My ticket also gave admission to the Palatine, the residence of emperors. This was an enormous site surrounded by beautiful gardens and several impressive buildings owned by different emperors. It was now late in the day, and I was feeling weary, so I made my way back to the Colosseum to see inside.

If the Colosseum was impressive from the outside, it was even more impressive inside. I could only hazard a guess at the circumference of the arena; it seemed to be at least ten times the area of the Sydney Showground. Three main tiers of seats stretching like a skyscraper into the sky, with a capacity of fifty-five thousand spectators. Innumerable entranceways with steps and corridors leading to the seating and three wide walkways separating the levels. This I knew from my teaching of ancient Rome. What I did not realise was the amount of underground structure that was beneath the surface of the arena. A vast series of deep stone tunnels covered the arena floor. Not surprising when you think about all the wild animals that were kept and used in the games, let alone the gladiators. You could even work out where the animals would have been released into the arena. I was mentally preparing my next lesson on ancient Rome.

As I made my way home, I was totally in school mode, how I could make what I had experienced real for my class; and although I had only spent three days in Rome, I had been so lucky to have had good weather and wonderful experiences.

CHAPTER 36

Backpacking in Paris

THE TRAIN FROM ROME to Paris took fourteen hours, with a change of trains near the Italian border. The cheapest and most convenient ticket would leave at 2.30pm and arrive in Paris at 6.30am, which would mean an overnight trip without the expense of a sleeper, but I felt sure I would be tired enough to sleep anyway. So I left my bag at the hostel reception and took another walk to the ancient centre to say goodbye to the real Rome.

Once on the train, I watched with interest the disappearing Italian countryside. It is funny how important it had become to remember this journey in Italy now that I was leaving, whereas when you are arriving, you are so anxious to get there that the countryside is not as important. In the early hours of the morning, I had to change trains and found no problem being able to sleep in my seat. The train terminated at the Gare de Lyon as I was awakened by the loud announcement.

Luckily, the station was only two blocks from the river Seine, and my address in the Latin Quarter was advertised as walking distance from the Notre-Dame, another high point of reference. Luckily too, I was told I could have a bed for three days, leave my bag there and return by three o'clock. Whereas I would dearly have loved to just go back to bed, I set off to visit my landmark, the Notre-Dame Cathedral.

I had not realised that the cathedral was built on an island in the Seine, but there were several bridges and jetties so that one could visit by boat. I approached from the east through a peaceful square and was initially impressed with the intricate construction. The main entrance was to the west, so I walked round and found not one, but three main entrances, each holding statues of saints and kings, above which was the most beautiful stained glass round window reflecting shades of red and blue and above that two bell towers and finally a huge spire coming from the centre of the building. Inside was dark, lit only by light from the rose windows, and as I strained my eyes to see, I could hear deep resonant chanting. Once again, I had the distinct feeling of weakness in the knees and a desperate need to sit down. So I felt my way to the back pews and sat, feeling overcome by the solemnity of the space and the power of the music. The mass chanting was followed by a monologue in a language that didn't sound French. I thought it might be Latin but was not sure. I couldn't see the narrator, or the massed choir, but I was held by a mysterious presence that I felt I could not disturb, so I sat and breathed in the experience. I couldn't wander around the interior of the cathedral. That felt disrespectful, and luckily for me, no other tourist entered while I was there, so I had my quasi-religious experience to myself.

Back outside, I set off to see the legendary Louvre Museum. If I hadn't already read that the Louvre had once been a royal palace, it was blatantly obvious just by the size and splendour of the building. Huge pillared colonnades, rows of statues, ornate designs on every surface, as I wandered around looking for the entrance. Finally, I found a sign stating that at this time the museum was closed for renovations. At least I found the Arc de Triomphe, so often portrayed in films made in Paris, and being the culture philistine I was at that time, it didn't bother me that although I had seen the Louvre, I hadn't actually been inside. I considered moving on to the Eiffel Tower, but it began to rain, and I had second thoughts about paying for a view that would be obscured by cloud. Maybe tomorrow would be better, so I settled for an enormous coffee with milk in a huge two-handled mug and a warm croissant. It seemed worth the extra price to be seated inside. The following day was grey but fine, so I set out to visit the Eiffel Tower. Because I was unsure of cutting across streets to reach my destination, I followed the river the long way round, but it was a very pleasant walk in the crisp, cool air. The tower is an impressive building, with its delicate patten of wrought-iron girders making it seem a mix of delicate and sturdy construction. Craning my neck to see the very top, with my dislike of heights, I decided to just visit the first level rather than the very top or third level. Also, my choice was cheaper. As I was standing in the queue, waiting for the lift, suddenly, it felt like winter. Even though I was wearing tights and woollen socks under my jeans and a winter singlet, skivvy, jumper, duffel coat, scarf and beanie, this was the first time I had really felt cold, colder than in snow-covered Switzerland! Once in the first level, Visitor Centre, the usual indoor heat was back, and worst of all, the floor was made of glass, so looking down was definitely dizzy making. So I probably didn't make the most of my visit.

Back down in the fresh air, I was thinking of walking through the adjacent gardens when I was approached by a young dark-skinned man, who greeted me politely in English, asking if I were an English visitor. When I said yes, he asked me if he could be my guide and practise his English. He said he could show me beautiful gardens, lovely buildings and monuments, all free of charge. His only payment would be the price of a coffee and picnic lunch. He asked me where I was staying and said he could deliver me to my home whenever I wished. I considered this offer for a moment. After all, it was still morning, bright daylight, I was in a tourist city where the sight of police was very evident, and I didn't have much money on me, so what real danger was there? I had my French phrase book in my bag and had learned useful phrases such as 'I am sorry I do not speak French very well', 'Please can you help me?', 'Where is the toilet/ station/river?', etc. All I had to do to find my way home was to follow the river Seine! I felt confident I could handle any situation.

So often I am quick to seize the moment, thinking that this seems a good idea at the time. Sometimes it is, but other times not. In my defence this time, I had been impressed by this man's gentle, polite manner. There was an air of poverty about him; he was certainly down-at-heel, with a lean frame and a gaunt look, but he had a quiet dignity in the way he offered his services and in wanting payment in food rather than money. The pickings must have been slim that morning at the Eiffel Tower as I must have looked somewhat down-at-heel also. My walking shoes had been well broken in before I left

Australia, and I had been travelling twelve days without washing my outer clothing.

So I said I was just thinking of walking through these gardens, and if he wanted to walk with me, that would be okay, and if he could point out another sight on my map and if it seemed wonderful, yes, I would buy him coffee. So we walked through the gardens which led to the military school, and he told me the history of the place, that the gardens had once been a military parade ground. He also told me he was Algerian, had come to France on a student visa many years ago, but wasn't a French citizen and so couldn't get work. He had studied languages and history; spoke French, English, German, a little Dutch and Italian; and would dearly love to be a registered guide, but racism was rife in France, and his skin was dark. As my home was in the Latin Quarter, he suggested we walk via the Invalids Area and then down to the Luxembourg Gardens and finally visit the Pantheon before arriving home. This sounded wonderful as I hadn't really planned much other than the places I had visited, wasn't particularly happy with the photocopied map I had and hadn't been able to find a tourist office to get a better one.

It certainly wasn't far to walk as the gardens adjacent to the Eiffel Tower led to the military school, which led to the Hôtel des Invalides or military hospital. My guide kept giving me historical information as we walked. The hospital was built by Louis XIV in the seventeenth century, the first military hospital for French war veterans. European royalty really made superb buildings. Although rather austere in decoration, as befits a military hospital, it was enormous in size, being four stories high and easily four times the length of the Queen Victoria Building in Sydney. The main entrance was more ornate, with carved statues on each pillar and engraved figures of mounted heroes on the top level, underneath a huge engraved arch. There appeared to be a tower topped by a glittering dome, rising from the centre. It really was an impressive sight, well worth the price of lunch. Of course, there was an entrance fee to see inside, but I was happy with just seeing the building. But that was not all; around the corner was St. Louis des Invalides, the soldiers' church. Once again, a plain building which apparently housed spoils of war, banners seized in battle. Next to that was the much more elaborate Dome des Invalides, a church, also built by Louis XIV, for the exclusive use of royalty and which became the location of royal tombs. This was a glorious white marble structure, the owner of the tower and dome I had seen from the entrance to Hotel des Invalides. Now the dome was clearly visible and reminded me of the dome of St Peters, Rome. My guide told me that mass was heard simultaneously in both churches so that the king and subjects worshipped simultaneously. He also mentioned that the Dome church held Napoleon's tomb as the little general had expressed a desire to be buried on the banks of the Seine.

Now we were to lunch in the Luxembourg Gardens, a reasonable walk away, but we would pass some interesting buildings on the way. I had never been on a guided walk before, so I had no reference to compare, but I was reminded of my days at the riding school, choosing a route to suit the specific clientele and indicating points of interest on the way. As we strolled along, Aadin, my guide, mentioned famous people who lived in the area. By this stage, we were on a first-name basis. Aadin meant first, and he was the eldest son. Then we paused at a little food store, and I bought coffee and baguettes filled with ham and cheese. Finally, we reached the gardens, fortunately free to enter, and what a beautifully peaceful haven it was. Just handfuls of strolling visitors, families with children, elderly couples and couples on bikes, all using the concrete paths than travelling beneath the forest of trees. It was wintertime, so the trees were not at their best. I would have loved to be there in the spring, but I would imagine there would be triple the number of visitors. Luckily, we were able to find two wrought-iron seats in the garden in front of the Luxembourg Palace, so as we ate our lunch, Aadin told me its history. It had been built by Marie de Medici, the widow of King Henry IV, who had been living in the palace at the Louvre. She was born in Florence, so her new palace reflected her ancestral home. She organised the extensive gardens, and the fountain we would see here is called Fontaine Medicis, styled like an Italian grotto.

The palace had an interesting modern history. After Marie's death, a public art gallery was included. During the French Revolution, it became a prison. Napoleon Bonaparte lived there and installed his ministry there. During the Second World War, Goring claimed it as the headquarters of the Luftwaffe and stayed there when he visited Paris. Today, it is home to the Senate of the Republic. I was so pleased I had visited Florence, and yes, I could see the resemblance to the magnificent Italian buildings and looked forward to seeing the fountain. But before we set off on our walk, Aadin had something serious to say. He felt that this morning walk had been adequately paid for by lunch, and he was committed to taking me home but asked if I would be interested in something extra. Internally, I felt my stomach clench as I waited. Had I made the wrong choice, after all? He already knew I was due to leave the following day, so what could he offer?

Well, he also knew I liked live music, folk, jazz, anything really that involved watching musicians play. Now the pitch: Would I like to watch live music and have a meal in the Latin Quarter tonight? He didn't know who would be playing or how good they would be, but the man who ran the establishment allowed the musicians a meal and a bed for the night, and as they were outcasts in this society and homeless, that was a good deal for them. To the other outcasts, illegal guides like himself, if their client paid an entry fee and paid for their meal as well as their own, he would have a bed for the night as well.

Once again, I had to think it over. I couldn't remember how much cash money I had, knowing I had cashed my last traveller's cheque. Where was this place, and would there be drunken outcasts aplenty? Would I be able to walk home late at night if Aadin was sleeping there? He could see I was hesitant and said,

'Okay, if you are unsure, do you want to walk there before it gets dark and meet the man in charge?'

That didn't make it any easier. Now I was imagining white slave traders or ransom notes to my family.

'Okay, I can see you are not happy with this. Can I ask you one more thing? You are going back to Australia, a land of sunshine.

Would you be happy to leave behind your woollen socks, clean or dirty, doesn't matter, maybe your scarf and beanie, if I walk you to the station tomorrow so you can wear them there?'

That wasn't a problem. My suitcase was already jam-packed; although the only purchases I made were the fur coat and the boots, brochures also took up space. I was already thinking he deserved a tip as I had been so impressed with what he had shown me and the knowledge he had shared. So I quickly replied that I would be happy to give him all my warm clothing and all the French money I had left – which wasn't very much, I hastened to add. By this time, we were back in the Latin Quarter, so I agreed to have a look at the establishment. It was only a couple of blocks from my accommodation, being in a rather rundown area, away from the Seine. There was a food shop on the ground level selling coffee and baguettes. Upstairs, the windows looked very similar to my place and, I guessed, were for paid accommodation, so where was the entertainment? Aadin spoke to the lady in charge, introduced me and asked if we could see inside. She led me through to the back of the kitchen, down a flight of stairs, and switched on a light, and there was a huge cavern with bare wooden floors, a drum kit and an old piano against one wall, while the other three walls held a motley assortment of chairs, sofas, beanbags and folded rugs. Aadin was talking rapidly to the woman who smiled, nodded and then spoke to me in English, saying,

'This is a very well-run place. My husband will not stand for any unseemly behaviour. If one of the boys becomes loving with a girl, he has to leave. Aadin will bring you here and take you home, but that will be early because we close at twelve and he could not get back in after that'.

She then told me the total cost, except drinks would be extra, and I said that I had to check how much I had and that I might see her later.

I really did have to calculate if I could afford a night out in Paris where I couldn't use my credit card, but I was convinced I could try. Once again, seize the moment. I would stay close to the door, and I knew my way home and could be out of there in an instant if a problem arose.

Fortunately, but mainly because I had been so frugal, I did have enough to pay the cost, give Aadin a tip and maybe have a drink or two (but only water). I would have no money then until I reached Australia, but the airline would cover food and sleep, and my credit card would cover costs in India. That, in fact, was true, but how it turned out was not what I had expected.

A quick change into a cotton shirt and comfortable shoes, a touch of lipstick and a brush of the hair and I was ready for a night out.

That was quite a night to remember. We were early, so we had a cup of coffee first while we waited for the room to open. The entrance was via a back lane, down steps and in by the wall that held the drums and piano. That was okay with me as I could say I like to be really close to the action and could guard my escape position. There definitely was a preponderance of males, mainly speaking French, several of whom greeted Aadin, smiled at me and headed for the bar. A group of young white men, Americans by their accent, arrived, and one asked me if I was English. He was amazed I was there alone, so I said, 'I am waiting for my boyfriend to come back'.

The room filled rapidly, and I had a problem maintaining my position as more musicians arrived and took pride of their place on that wall. Such a variety of people and instruments: from maracas, tambourines, castanets and every kind of percussion instrument to guitar, banjo, mouth organ, in fact any instrument that could be easily carried. Some arrived as couples and began to play, and then someone else would join them; it seemed totally unorganised, but they made interesting music. West Indian reggae, soulful blues and foot-stomping rock.

In no time at all, dinner was served, that is, Aadin went to the bar and returned with a bowl of what looked to be bean stew with a slice of bread.

At first, no one danced, and then a young girl in a flowing skirt and scarf began a gypsy-like dance, and others joined in, men and women. I was just happy to watch, with Aadin next to me happily chatting with his friends. Interestingly, although the place was crowded, the bar sold alcohol, and the music was exciting, I saw no drunken revellers, and I was not approached by anyone. By ten o'clock, I was ready to leave. Although I hadn't danced, it was really an interesting night.

Next morning, I had repacked my bag and had a bundle of warm things inside my laundry bag to give to Aadin, along with his tip. We walked via another park, Jardin des Plantes, a place I had missed entirely when I arrived, and then down to Gare de Lyon, from where I would catch the train to the airport. My flight was not until twelve thirty, so I wondered why Aadin wanted to get to the station so early. I thought he must be glad to see the back of me, but no, he had a surprise.

'Do you have a spare five franc?' he asked. 'Would you like to have a shower before your flight?'

Would I ever! None of my cheap accommodation in Europe had had a shower. Sometimes a shared bathroom with bath, sometimes just a basin of water. Apparently, Gare de Lyon had shower rooms, which is where the homeless shower if they have a spare five franc. Aadin knew the attendant, propelled me to the top of the ladies' queue and handed me a towel and soap. His reward was my beanie, socks and scarf, plus all the francs I had left as a tip.

CHAPTER 37

Stranded in Bombay

FINALLY ON BOARD AIR India flight to Bombay. Now I started to realise my predicament. I was still wait-listed from Bombay to Sydney. I would have to leave the airport at Bombay and try to find another flight home. Well, at least, I had been able to enjoy my European holiday, and although I didn't have any money, I had a credit card, and food on the plane was free. The plane travelled from Paris to Frankfurt, then on to Bombay, and who should join the plane at Frankfurt but a lad who had been in year 12 at Narrabeen High School in 1980. He was with his parents and younger brother, and they had just finished their European holiday, skiing and doing the Black Forest. They were returning as the younger brother was about to enter year 10 at Narrabeen High. I hadn't recognised him as year 9 students do not frequent the library as often as year 12. They were amazed that I was leaving the plane in Bombay and probably thought I was taking a long service leave holiday. I was amazed that they had bought their ticket much later than mine. Now I was starting to learn about the perils of a cheap ticket; if it is too good to be true, it probably isn't.

Bombay at last. I was clutching my last bottle of water, courtesy of Air India, as I collected my baggage and went through customs and out into the arrivals area, which was seething with humanity. I couldn't see a help desk to arrange accommodation, so I headed for the exit doors to be immediately grabbed at by seemingly dozens of Indian men. Shaking them off, I stumbled back through the exit door, deciding I needed to stay at the airport to sort out my return flight. I wandered through the arrivals area, looking for help, and finally found an Air India lady who spoke English. She was very sympathetic as she heard my story, but very definite in her reply.

'You have a restricted ticket, only available for certain times of the year when we are not too busy. Right now, it is our busiest time of year to Australia, so you could not use this ticket before the tenth of February. You have two options: organise your return flight with us today and spend some time in Bombay or try the other airlines to see if you can find an earlier ticket to Australia. All the airlines have offices in the floors above, but they will not be open until nine. In the meantime, you can stay in the transit lounge'. She pointed me in that direction. I checked my watch against hers; it was a quarter to two in the morning!

Then I realised Reg was expecting me to collect Greg on the weekend. It was now Wednesday morning, and I had little chance of making it home on time. When I asked if I could make a phone call to Australia, she replied,

'We have no access to Australian phones, only London. Do you have relatives there who could call Australia for you?'

Of course, I had an English passport; why wouldn't I have someone who could do this for me? Although I had several relatives in England, I hadn't been in touch for years; my mother did all the family updating. I didn't even have addresses, let alone phone numbers. So there was nothing I could do, knowing Reg might be concerned, but he would still keep Greg and would not worry about him missing a few days of school.

The transit lounge was fairly empty, only one white face visible and remarkable, a girl in her twenties, in a wheelchair, with a plastered foot.

I rushed over to say hello and hear her story as she was obviously in a worse situation than I was. Her name was Janice; she was going home to Melbourne, having been on a holiday in Goa with three other friends. Two of her friends had left for London, and what had been her boyfriend had stayed in Goa. She had broken her ankle falling down steps at Goa airport and had missed her flight. Airport officials had organised medical treatment and a flight to Bombay, but she had to arrange another flight to Melbourne as flights to Australia were full until the middle of February. So we were in the same predicament, and I could help her by pushing her wheelchair. She was ecstatic at my suggestion, even though I told her it was in my interest as well. I did feel rather stupid when I told her I had no money, only a credit card, but she said she would share what she had, and at least we could both use cards to buy our tickets.

Shortly after, everyone, except Janice and I, left the lounge for an unknown destination, and we continued to exchange details of our lives and travels. We were still lost in conversation when a large contingent of travellers arrived, so many that they completely filled the transit lounge. An announcement was made that the first-class lounge had been opened for those passengers awaiting transport to hotel accommodation. Janice and I wished we too could move to the first-class lounge.

Among the new arrivals left in transit was a young white girl with a dark-coloured baby, about a year old, who was obviously tired and fretful. I pushed Janice over, and we said hello and tried to distract the baby. The mother's name was Margaret and was hoping to get to Adelaide, back home to her parents. She had fallen in love with a Kenyan against the wishes of her parents, travelled to Kenya with him, had fallen pregnant and had a baby boy thirteen months ago. The marriage had become abusive, so she contacted her parents, and they had said,

'Get on the first plane you can and come home'.

She was in the same situation as Janice and I, needing to find a flight to Australia, but saddled with a baby, who at least would fly free on her lap. However, she had a lucky break; a middle-aged Australian couple came back to the transit lounge and found her, saying,

'Come with us. We will smuggle you into our hotel. This is an outrageous situation. Air India is responsible for missing our connecting flight, and it is simply appalling that they would leave a mother and baby without accommodation for over twenty-four hours in an airport lounge. There are usually two beds in a double room, in case couples prefer to sleep apart, so you will have a bed for you and the boy, and you can use their towels for nappies while we are there. If anyone objects, I will tell them I am going to make an official complaint and will see that the matter is handled legally'.

So forceful was he, with his wife picking up her luggage, Margaret couldn't refuse; and smiling good luck to us, she went with her saviours.

Nine o'clock next morning found us in a long corridor of offices of every airline I knew and many I didn't. Slowly, we made our way into each and every one, at first asking for flights to Australia, with no luck whatsoever. Then we refined our choice to Singapore, thinking maybe there will be more flights to Australia from there. Finally, we scored tickets to Singapore with Lufthansa, but not until Saturday morning. Fortunately, we both had enough credit on our cards to cover that cost and hopefully enough for the next flight as well. Back to the transit lounge for another night, but on the way, we found the first-class lounge unopen, but unlocked, so we entered and found a more comfortable room with a nicer toilet and comfortable seats.

I hadn't eaten for over twenty-four hours but hadn't really wanted to, feeling sick in the stomach with worry. Now we decided to enjoy our comfortable lounge until we were kicked out, and then we would go and find food. We didn't have our new home for long, but the very nice attendant said we could return after the entitled passengers left. Our new tickets earned us entry to the food court, but Indian airport food did not look or smell appetising, so we settled for samosas and water. I told Janice I would buy the food in Singapore using my credit card. Friday stretched ahead as we each told tales of our travels and life history. I was really missing something to read as all my printed materials had been jettisoned in Paris. We continued to ricochet between first-class and transit lounges until it was time to board the eight-hour Lufthansa flight to Singapore. Never had I been so ready to enjoy aircraft food. Never had I been so embarrassed by my appearance. I had worn my clothes for seventy-two hours non-stop; I was sure I smelt. My hair needed washing, my shoes retained the all-pervasive air of India, and my entire demeanour was one of helpless homelessness.

By comparison, the Lufthansa staff were immaculately attired and cloaked in a soft air of expensive European perfume and were totally masters of our fate.

Singapore airport was a joy to behold. So many beautiful flowers, dazzling shops, delicious-looking food and space to walk around, not hemmed in by humanity. Once again, we were too late to visit the airline offices, so we would have to spend the night at the airport, but what a wonderfully clean airport to spend the night. We could have a shower, wash our hair, change our clothes and feel bona fide travellers again, not forgotten dregs of the earth. The transit lounge even had sofas to stretch out on – luxury! The following morning, we headed for the Qantas office. Here I was introduced to the concept of standby fare, something cheapskate travellers relied on back in the day. I was a novice, and for me, the whole experience was daunting. I had to pay a set amount for a ticket to Sydney, look at the flights listed to leave and then wait at the gate as ticketed passengers boarded. Then if there was a spare seat, a cancellation or simply unpurchased, names of standby passengers would be read out, and they could then board.

As I stood at the gate, watching the lucky passengers boarding, I vowed I would never travel like this again. Holding my breath, I waited for the man to bring the list of the fortunate, praying I would be included. When he read out my name, head down, I literally ran forward, no thought about the girl with the baby or the girl with the broken ankle; I was getting onto that plane regardless.

What a contrast between the Lufthansa and the Qantas crew, the first so polite, so correct, so efficient, and the latter so cheery, so informal, so sloppy with language; I fell in love with Australia all over again.

I arrived home on the second of February. Greg was four days late for school.

CHAPTER 38

Life as a Single Mum

BACK IN AUSTRALIA, I had a massive credit card debt, but at least my regular salary had gone into my account and had paid my mortgage. Now I was in a very common situation for first-time credit card owners. When the bill arrived, I could not afford to pay the entire amount, so I paid as much as I could, thinking this is going to take years to discharge. The problem was I had already decided I wanted to spend next Xmas in Switzerland and take Greg with me. That, of course, depended on Michael adapting to boarding school and staying the full year. There was another need for money. I wanted to extend my house to enable the boys to have a bedroom each, and I too could have a room of my own and not sleep on the lounge anymore. To this end, I had already found a builder – by accident really. Reg had found another lady, so he no longer visited, forcing himself on me. I guess it had taken several months, but then I found myself missing male companionship and sex. When I first left home, the usual 'in with a chance' friends of Reg would visit and chat until I asked them to leave, and eventually, they gave up calling.

All except one: John Morgan, whom I had met the first night Reg had taken me to dinner at the restaurant frequented by cab drivers. He and his lovely wife, Val, had minded both boys, but particularly Michael, when I needed a babysitter and were often visitors at our place as we were at theirs. John, being a taxi driver, began to drop in at night when I lived in Balgowlah, and he was very good at listening to my troubles as he had seen the dark side of Reg from when he was married to Marg. I was surprised when John voiced the opinion that Reg had treated me very badly. I hadn't realised how my marriage looked from the outside. I began to rely on being able to share a problem with him, and he gave sound advice.

I didn't think I would see him again when I moved to Avalon, but occasionally, when he had a fare in that direction, he would pop in. As the only place to sit and talk was either the dining room or the lounge room, both being either side of the boys' bedroom, to avoid disturbing them, John and I would sit outside on the grass, drinking tea and having long, in-depth conversations about world events and current encounters. If I had had a difficult week and was feeling emotional, John would put his arm around me and give me a hug or perhaps a kiss on the head or cheek as he left. We were no more intimate than that. I hadn't particularly liked him originally as he seemed lecherous, but at this stage of our lives, we were just good friends, and I looked forward to our conversations. Unfortunately, unbeknown to us, Michael must have woken one night, come out to our outside toilet and noticed me with someone on the grass. He didn't disturb us. I didn't notice him, but he saw the taxi parked under the street light. So the next time he visited his father, he told him that John Morgan visits me late at night.

Reg then told Val, John's wife, that her husband was having an affair with me.

The next day, John was waiting for me after school and said that Val was leaving him. He had refused to move out as he hadn't done anything wrong, so she was moving into a flat in Manly. I was horrified at my welcoming his visits, my son not confronting me first and Reg telling Val something that was not true. That was it; as far as I was concerned, John could not visit me ever again. Unfortunately, John was very concerned about me, worrying that Reg could turn nasty. We agreed that phone calls would be our only means of communication.

I penned a letter to Val stating that we were not having an affair, just that John had visited late one night on his way back from a fare to Palm Beach and had a cup of tea and we sat in the backyard to not disturb the boys. Obviously, one had seen the taxi and told Reg.

Some weeks later, I received a short note from Val, saying,

'Do not contact me again. You say you believe in human rights and then take my lifeline away. You have lost nothing. I have lost the relationship with my husband and two little boys I have known since birth and love dearly'.

When Reg came to bring the boys home, he abused me and took a swing at me, but I ducked, and he punched his hand through my lounge room wall. So I would live with the memory of that whole fiasco all the time I lived in Avalon. Reg also assured me he was going to divorce me, citing John Morgan as co-respondent, and would see the boys were banned from having any connection with him. Even though in the three years we had been separated, Reg had had two successive ladies share his bed. Some two years later, that was exactly what he did. My friends had urged me to get divorced as a current husband was entitled to half of my house. On my wage, I could not get legal aid, so I couldn't afford a divorce. Reg, on the other hand, had been contacted by Else, one of the Dutch girls who had gone boating with him back in 1970. She was in Australia, had heard that I had left home and was wondering if he were divorced. If so, she asked if he would like to marry her so that she could stay in Australia, and she was prepared to pay him $1,000 for the privilege. She would place no limits on the arrangement; only it was necessary to live together for long enough to convince immigration authorities that her story was true. Her records proved she had been in Sydney in 1970, where she claimed they had had an affair. When she heard I had left, she contacted Reg, and the passion flared again. I had refused to give Reg a divorce, but now he had evidence I had another man, so he could divorce me.

Back to my builder, in 1979 and the good old days of the local paper *The Manly Daily*, which I would read from cover to cover. One day in the 'Men Wanting Women' section, I read,

'Working builder, family man with two daughters, three dogs and a horse, seeks lady for companionship and outings. Location Avalon!'

Well, it was worth a phone call. What did I have to lose? We met for coffee in Avalon, and then he took me to his rented house to meet his daughters and animals. Apparently, his previous house, which he had built, had been sold in the divorce, but his girls, aged in their early twenties, had opted to live with him rather than their mother, who was living with her boyfriend. This all sounded very positive, and the girls were very pleased to meet me. I told him that I worked virtually seven days a week, but it would be lovely to have a meal out occasionally.

Slowly, the friendship with Bob developed, but I would have to be sure my boys were happy with that as I had only been separated two years and was not divorced.

The boys were happy with the association as they could see the house extension was a possibility. Bob's daughters had also contacted me early in the piece to fill me in on their dad's problems. He had been devastated by his wife's departure and had lost his dream house and his work because he had taken to the bottle, drinking himself into a stupor at night and being unable to get to work in the morning. They were endeavouring to look after him, but they felt a new lady in his life was the tonic he needed to turn his life around. I wasn't sure I could achieve the miracle they hoped for as I hadn't had another man in my life for three years and wasn't really sure if I wanted one. Realistically, I had little time to offer; teaching at Narrabeen High School and the riding school took up all my days. However, as I was a librarian at Narrabeen, I was spared the nightly chore of preparation and marking, so I could offer an evening meal and companionship for a couple of hours. Having the boys in the only bedroom and my bed on the lounge meant little chance of an intimate relationship. The girls also urged me to ask Bob to build the extension as he was well qualified to do that and it would give him purpose and a working environment again.

So that was how I came to lodge an application as owner-builder for an extension that would double the size of the house, adding two bedrooms, a rumpus room and a second bathroom with toilet for whenever sewerage came to Avalon. My mortgage had been with a different bank to mine, one, the real estate agent had convinced me, that would lend the money. My Westpac bank, which had handled my money since I turned sixteen, had refused to lend me $300 to fix my car back in 1976 and also refused a personal loan of $10,000 I asked for. The very apologetic bank manager suggested I try NRMA, and based on my membership since 1968 and my teacher's salary, they agreed. All of this had been achieved the previous year, and Bob was anxious to start. He had also been expecting he would have my company for the six-week holiday and was quite upset when he learned I would be away for four weeks.

When I returned, I learned from his daughters that he had completely fallen off the wagon and they had left home! His situation was so bad that I insisted he needed to go to a rehabilitation place in Fairlight for a week to dry out before I would see him, and he did, being virtually homeless. Fortunately, help was at hand. He stayed at Fairlight for another week and then was found subsidised accommodation in Mona Vale.

The $10,000 I had borrowed would cover building costs, and I would cover the living costs, buying groceries and filling the car, so there was no cash in hand to spend on booze. I made a detailed spreadsheet listing credit due for work and debit for costs and said I would repay his work payment at a later date or if he quit.

In the weeks and months that followed, my house grew. Greg was quite interested in the whole process and often spent weekends helping. I vividly remember the weekend the floorboards were laid. I didn't realise every floorboard was laid and then re-laid, carefully brushing any dust away. Karen's boyfriend, now husband, Paul, was a plasterer and volunteered his services, and his friend was an electrician who did the same at 'mate's rates'. My part of the deal was to pay for materials and supply lunch on the days they worked. My finances were stretched, and I became expert at 101 ways with mince.

Michael had been told if he became too homesick and unhappy in boarding school he could come home at the end of the school year, which was the start of the summer holidays. If he wanted to stay, he had to return at Easter the following year to join the Australian education system to do his school certificate. Phillip thought one year would be enough for him but underestimated Michael's persistence. I thought there was every likelihood that Michael would want to stay until next year, and if so, I wanted to give Greg the opportunity to travel overseas. I knew that if he left before his twelfth birthday on 3 December, I could get his return fare for half price, so hopefully, by severely restricting my budget, I could do that. Not a windmill European visit, but a trip to London to stay with relatives and visit the Tower of London and two weeks in Switzerland, staying in Phillip's apartment, with his brother showing him how to ski.

This, in fact, was how the plan worked out, organising tickets with Air Italia, leaving on 27 November and returning on 23 January. Greg seemed interested in seeing Rome. I think there may have been a movie or TV series that featured fast Alfa cars and police using machine guns that sparked his interest, so I allowed for two nights in Rome. Our itinerary was to spend two weeks in London, catch the ferry to France, spend two nights in Paris, visit the Eiffel Tower, take the train to Geneva and stay with the Pagets for three days. Then we would use Phillip's car to drive to Gstaad and have two weeks with Michael and finally drive back to Geneva and take the train to Rome.

My house extension grew very slowly. When Bob needed an extra tradesman to help, he had to find a mate, preferably one who didn't have a job so that he could spend the time. I really couldn't afford another wage, so if Paul wasn't available, often the job would stay idle for days. Keeping to his Alcoholics Anonymous pledge, Bob would work in my garden or take his dogs for a run at Palm Beach at these times. Greg was really fond of the youngest dog, a blue cattle, called Ernie. Our old foxie Stumpy had gone to doggy heaven the previous year.

It was rather a tragic ending; I inadvertently ran over him, not knowing he was under the car. He dragged himself off to die, and Greg grabbed him and wrapped him in the towel which was always on the back seat, and I drove us to the Avalon Vet. Tears streaming down our faces, Greg and I presented at the surgery, knowing our dog was about to be put down. He was fourteen years old and had been the runt of the litter, not immediately available for sale, and now he was almost blind and so stiff with arthritis, he needed help to get up the single step into the house. I had felt the bump as the wheel of the car went over him. After examining him, the vet announced,

'It is probably a broken pelvis. I will X-ray to be sure, and then we will fit him with a cast'.

I could not believe my ears.

'This is an old dog, nearly blind and crippled with arthritis. You are surely not going to make him wear a cast?'

'Blind dogs can manage quite well, and I can give him an injection for his arthritis' was his reply.

'No', I said, 'I don't want him to suffer anymore'.

'Well, if you just want to put him down, okay, we will send you a bill'.

With that, he picked up the dog and left. Greg and I hugged each other and left as well.

We hadn't been ready to get another dog as we already had a cat, a ginger kitten Greg had brought home and named Custard, saying,

'I like custard, and I like this kitten'.

I must note here that I did make many custards, so much so that Greg would ask,

'What is for custard instead of what is for dessert?'

When Ernie became a regular visitor, Custard decided she didn't want to share the household with a dog, and so she left home for next door, where there were two compatible old cats. My next-door neighbours were a retired couple who lived in a large garage with windows. There wasn't a fence between our properties; neither of us could afford one as the backyard was extensive. Our dog wouldn't venture into their yard because their cats were not so accommodating, but our cat would often spend the day there and finally decided to eat there as well. I began buying cat food and leaving it next door.

Bob noticed that Greg had taken a liking to Ernie, and as he really wasn't allowed a dog at his new premises because his daughters had already taken one dog, Bob kept his old dog and gave Ernie to Greg. Ernie was a very smart dog and learned all the games Greg and his friends played, such as cricket, soccer and hide-and-seek. He knew the rules: whom to bring the cricket ball to, who to keep away from the soccer ball, etc. That summer, he even tried riding a surfboard and jumping off the pier, but hide-and-seek was his speciality. Up in the sandhills of Palm Beach, no one could successfully evade his nose.

By Easter, the extension was nearly finished, and Michael had written and said he would really like to stay in Switzerland for the winter term, returning the following Easter, and asked if Greg could come with me to visit over Christmas. Phillip agreed but didn't offer me a ticket this time. Could I raise the money? It is amazing what having a credit card can tempt you to do. Greg was anxious to have the opportunity to do a real skiing holiday, so I maxed out my credit card and raised the cost of riding tuition. I thought I would just keep paying the minimal amount forever to take advantage of this opportunity. Phillip did offer accommodation in his London apartment, so I contacted my mum for my numerous London relatives and contacted them to say we were coming. I had kept contact with the Paget family, so there would be accommodation in Geneva, and Phillip offered his car for the drive to Gstaad.

All seemed well, until sometime in September, Greg seemed to be having second thoughts about the trip. I could not understand why and thought maybe Reg had influenced him. It was not until Greg's birthday that I discovered the truth. We were due to fly out on 27 November, six days before Greg's birthday, and Greg had been adamant that he wanted a birthday party as it would be the last time he would see some of his friends. Apparently, many Avalon parents, having been quite satisfied with public education in primary school, tended to opt for private education in high school. I always took the day off to host his birthday party, and the previous year, he had a limit of eleven friends. This year, I offered a compromise. We had to have the party early as we were due to fly out. Flushed with my ability to use credit, I would fund a trip to Luna Park, but only for four as that was the car's capacity. He was very happy with this arrangement, and I left him to offer invitations.

Little did I realise the chosen four would be his best buddy and two girls! Last year, it had been manly boys and an odd couple of girls playing chasings and hide-and-seek with Ernie at Palm Beach. Michael hadn't noticed girls in primary school, but obviously, Greg had. On the way home in the car, the girls lamented that Greg was going to miss the year 6 formal! I didn't realise year 6 had a formal! Who would Tammie dance with now that Greg wouldn't be there? I didn't realise primary-age children danced together! At least now we both could get excited about the trip to Europe.

CHAPTER 39

1982 – Second Trip to Europe

AFTER A GRUELLING TWENTY-FOUR-HOUR Air Alitalia flight to London, we took a taxi to Phillip's apartment and met the lovely next-door neighbours who had a son about the same age as Greg. When I mentioned I would be visiting my relatives who lived in New Cross, they seemed worried about me and said,

'Be careful, that is not a safe area to walk about on your own'. I replied that I would go on the metro and my relatives would pick me up from the station.

Greg and I made the trip to meet the dozens of relatives who turned out to greet us. I thought at the time that it should have been my mum here meeting her relatives and wondered if someday in the future, I could save up and bring her back to London. Interestingly, when one of the cousins drove us home that evening, his parting words were

'Be careful here. It is not really a safe place to wander alone'.

It made me think, 'Does everyone in London believe that every suburb is not safe to walk alone?'

But wander we did to see Buckingham Palace, where Greg was disappointed that we couldn't see inside, and the Tower of London, where we could go inside and see the crown jewels and the place where even royalty had their heads cut off. Most impressive were the guards with their distinctive headgear. Greg thought they must be making a film and had dressed up for the part.

Then we were off to catch the train, ferry and train to Paris.

A very short stay in Paris, just to climb the Eiffel Tower and walk into Notre Dame, and then it was another train to Geneva. Here we stayed with the Pagets for two days, and then I drove Phillip's car to Saanen. This was my first experience of driving on the right-hand side of the road, which was a little unnerving. Even more frightening was when I met a train coming towards me on my side of the road and had to quickly move to the left. I had thought the road seemed a little uneven but hadn't realised I had been travelling along train tracks and would continue to do so for some miles! However, it was a beautiful scenery, so lush and green, with picturesque two-storey wooded chalets with steeply sloping rooves and purple mountains in the distance. I could tell that Greg was impressed by this new country as he remarked,

'I thought Switzerland was totally snow covered'.

'Well, it will be in weeks. That is why Michael wanted to stay for the holidays and take you skiing'.

Finally, we reached the homestead and were greeted by the owner, who gave Greg a hug and said, 'I can see he is like his brother', a fact I hadn't noticed. They had a grandson, Stephan, staying for the Christmas holidays, but he spoke mainly German, a little French and less English. It was interesting watching the boys play and make themselves understood with much mime and gesture. When I collected Michael from school, I discovered he had grown so much in the past year that he had acquired a new parka, so fortunately, his old one would now be Greg's. We spent Christmas with the Bach family, walking down to the little church for midnight mass, carrying candles which we left on the graves. Back at home, we could watch the flickering lights beneath us like a magical fairyland.

The Bach family Christmas was a very German affair with roast goose with potato dumplings and red cabbage, followed by cherry compote Christmas stollen and gingerbread cookies. On Boxing Day, Michael set about teaching Greg the basics in skiing, although real snow had not yet fallen.

What a magical morning the day the snow arrived. Sparkling white covering everything, the tiny church looking its best with a snow-covered roof. Michael had to return to school, but Phillip had arranged for Robert, the boy from the next-door London family, to come and spend a week in Saanen and take skiing lessons with Greg. What a wonderful holiday for both my boys!

CHAPTER 40

1984 – The Family Together Again

MICHAEL RETURNED TO AUSTRALIA and to Barrenjoey High School in term 2 and threw himself back into surfing. The house extension had been finished, and both boys had a room each, and so did I. Now I was to find problems with having a larger house that I had not anticipated. It seemed only a short time that he had been at home when I discovered a girl in Michael's bed. This would have been impossible back in the day when I locked both outside doors and went to bed later than the boys. Now it was so easy for Michael to leave the back door unlocked, and with me in the front room and them in the farthest back room, I was totally unaware. I was outraged and angry, although they did look so sweet, wrapped up together in a single bed. I demanded to know whether they had taken precautions and if they realised that what they were doing was breaking the law, an actual criminal offence on Michael's part. The girl, Michelle, was so embarrassed, while Michael was surprised I was reacting in this way.

'It's only natural when you love someone, Mum'.

'Well, I don't want to have this happening under my roof when I bet Michelle's mother doesn't know. Where does she think you are, young lady?'

Michelle didn't answer me; she just snuggled farther down under the doona.

'Well, you had better get up and dressed as I am driving you home to tell your mother'.

As I stormed back downstairs, I caught a fleeting glance of the girl dashing out the back door, running for home.

So I confronted my son.

'Is this the first time this had happened with Michelle, and did you take precautions?'

'Well, it is the first time we have spent the whole night together, but not the first time we have had sex. Yes, we did take precautions. I was given contraceptives at school when we had our sex education lectures'.

'Europe must have lowered the age of consent because in Australia, it is still sixteen. Four months away, and I bet Michelle is only fifteen at the most. I need to know if her parents consented to her being sexually involved with you, even if you are taking precautions. I need to know her last name and phone number so I can have that conversation'.

'Mum, you know I can't do that. She would be in a lot of trouble. I don't want her to be hurt. I won't do this again, but please don't involve her parents'.

'Have you met her parents?' I asked.

'Yes, I have, and they are both very strict. It was just that Greg was going to stay with Reg this weekend that I thought it would be a good idea, but I didn't really think she would do it'.

Then we had the birds and the bees talk, how a body is primed to reproduce and as soon as a child is physically mature enough, the body encourages this, even though that same child might not be emotionally or psychologically ready for the possibilities. I warned Michael,

'Although you may feel you truly love this girl and your body is urging you to take the next step towards fulfillment of that desire, a consideration of the ultimate results of that step should make you pause. After all, the law of the land states that sexual intimacy is forbidden to those under sixteen, which both of you are. If the girl's parents want to lay charges against you that you have sexually abused their daughter, you, being the older party, are responsible for your actions. You really do need to consider all the ramifications of the sexual act, not just rush in because it feels good. Even if you are sure both of you are truly in love, if you don't care that you could create a baby, be very careful. Once that baby arrives, there is no love as powerful as the love of a mother for her child. It will far exceed the love for her partner, and if you have not totally committed to this undertaking, she will leave you to defend her baby. You have already taken the big step in this case, but you have not consulted her parents, and the threat of prosecution hangs over you. If you continue to indulge, could the time come when you are so intent on gratification that you forget to use protection? To me, if a girl is sexually active, she should be on the contraceptive pill, but I don't know what the ethics are of GPs in general. Is it against their moral code to prescribe the pill to an underage girl? I would truly like to have a conversation with her mother about where we should go from here. I assume you became sexually active in Switzerland, and I hope you took care to take precautions'.

'Yes, Mum, the girls wouldn't do it unless you wore a rubber. None of them wanted to get pregnant, but they were anxious to have sex'.

'With no parents around to have the conversation with, I bet the teachers would not have been happy to know about sexual relations among the students'.

'I think they probably knew, just didn't want anyone to fall pregnant', Michael replied.

'That is the problem. Because the most likely time a girl will fall pregnant is her very first time because this is the culmination of her body's race to maturity. So if you are the least bit careless in preparation and withdrawal, it is likely to happen, and life will dramatically change for both of you. Fifteen and sixteen is far too young to be faced with this problem, so it is totally unfair to take advantage of a young girl who is at the mercy of her emotions when you can probably satisfy your needs yourself!'

Michael blushed at this thought but kept his thoughts to himself.

'Finally, I would like to have a conversation with her mum and need the information to do that. In the meantime, I do not want her or any other girl in this house until I have been introduced to them and know their parents, and I want you to consider what you are going to say and do with Michelle in future'.

Just to make sure, I moved my bed into the back rumpus room and guarded the back door from intruders. Some months later, when Michael's sixteenth birthday loomed near, he said he was having a combined birthday party with another girl from school, whose parents were paying big money to hire Whale Beach Surf Club for the night to hold an alcohol-free fancy dress disco night. Narrabeen High School was planning a musical, *Dracula Spectacular*, so I was able to borrow the lead actor's costume for this occasion and met Michelle, going as a baby, and drove them there and collected them afterwards.

CHAPTER 41

1984 – The Birthday I Would Never Forget

BY THE END OF year 10, Michael was most unhappy with Barrenjoey High, even though he had a starring role, playing Freddie Belvedere in the play *Baby You're the Cat's Pyjamas*. I wasn't sure how much pressure he was under from his peers as the year overseas had added a little polish to his speech and attitudes. Did his friendship with Phillip attract condemnation or criticism? What Michael told me was that he was tired of running the French class as he was just so much better than all the others. He felt that the school lacked ambition for students to really succeed and that just coping and being comfortable with studies was the norm rather than stretching and excelling. He began to push to change to a more rigorous private school. To me, this was totally impossible, and even if I had the money, I was still dedicated to public education. Phillip, on the other hand, was so impressed with Michael's attitude that he wanted him to have the opportunity. Boarding school was ruled out, but I was not prepared to move and disturb Greg, who seemed happy at Barrenjoey. Then suddenly, there appeared a possibility. Matthew, the surfing boy from Manly, had moved with his girlfriend to the city suburb of Waterloo. If Michael could get into Sydney Grammar, he could stay with them Monday to Friday and come home to me on weekends and holidays. Michael was ecstatic at the idea and luckily was able to get into Sydney Grammar. I think his year in Switzerland helped there. Once again, Michael leapt at the challenge to excel, telling me, 'You haven't seen the best of me yet, but now you will'.

He seemed to make friends easily and would bring home a mate to have a surfing weekend in Avalon.

In the summer of 1984, my forty-third birthday was approaching. Somehow, one can steel yourself ready for the big fortieth birthday, chanting 'Life begins at 40' and planning for the next exciting decade of your life, but as you hit forty-one, forty-two, and now forty-three, nothing has really changed. I am still a single mother working two jobs, raising two boys, with only negative input from their father. Enthusiasm for this new decade in my life has totally dissolved.

My eldest son had enticed me to take the Saturday (my birthday) off from the riding school where I worked as he had a special surprise for me. My younger son already had a party engagement that day but had assured me he would be home for the cutting of my cake that evening.

The morning dawned bright and clear as I, still in bed, took my breakfast tray, artfully adorned with frangipani flowers floating in a saucer, a boiled egg with buttered soldiers and a portion of the Sydney Morning Herald, open at the advertisements. I wondered at the trouble the boys had taken.

'We have planned a special day out for you, Mum. After breakfast, we are going on a drive to visit horses for sale. I have marked them out in the paper. We can pretend we are looking to buy and have a ride on unknown animals. We can do lunch somewhere on the road and come home to pizza and cake for dinner, my treat. You won't have to do anything today. I'll drive!'

Suddenly, I understood. My seventeen-year-old son had passed his Ls and was desperate to log the driving kilometres before he sat the real driving test. What a great opportunity for him, making his mum happy too, a win-win situation.

Except that I actually loathed sitting next to a learner driver. I had presumed his father would do this chore, but he had flown back to the country town from whence he came, and the boys had to go there to see him.

But when your child is beaming with excitement and joy at his own brilliance in cheering up his grumpy mum, what could I say?

'What a lovely idea. I had better make some phone calls'.

So we set out. First stop, Terrey Hills, to ride a very stroppy pony with a mouth of iron and a sneaky temperament, trying to take the rider under trees or close to the fence to try and scrape them off. I didn't bother to say that I'll think about it and just advised the owner that she really needed a trainer to make the pony presentable. Next stop, St. Ives, to a lovely thoroughbred housed in a stable with his own training yard. He would have done well in his younger days, but a quick look at his teeth revealed he was much more than the ten years advertised; together with the stiffness in his gait and heavy breathing after cantering, it showed he really didn't have too many years left on this earth.

Actually, I found myself enjoying, testing my skills at picking faults and bursting with pride at my child's competence in riding, and his driving wasn't that bad either, but the traffic was quite light.

Two more stops somewhere out west to see very uninteresting horses, lunch at a hamburger place, and now the traffic was increasing.

'I think we have done enough now. Let's head home,' I suggested.

'Oh, Mum, there is just one more. It is not far to Bringelly, and this is an Arab, your favourite horse'.

That did perk my interest, so we continued to Bringelly.

As Michael drove up the driveway, I saw the most beautiful chestnut head looking over the gate and gazing with interest at us. It was love at first sight. All previous thoughts of 'Let's go home' vanished. I just wanted to stroke that lovely neck and breathe her in.

A middle-aged man answered my knock and said,

'She is my daughter's horse, but I don't think she really wants to sell her as she has knocked back three prospective buyers. You can have a ride if you like, but you will have to ring her to see if she wants to sell the mare as she has gone home'.

A later conversation revealed that his daughter had bought the horse as a yearling, he had broken the mare in, and it had been the pet of the family for three years, never going off the property. Now his daughter was married and pregnant and felt she could not give the horse the life it deserved.

As I rode the horse around the yard, I was in heaven. She was so responsive, eager to look about and with a long striding pace. When I watched Michael riding her, she seemed to float across the ground, head held high, mane waving, tail arched in a high plume. She was everything I had ever dreamed about. I took the phone number, saying I would contact the daughter, and stroked the mare farewell. On the drive home, I could not get the feel of that horse out of my head.

'What a pity I can't afford to buy that horse. She is absolutely perfect in every way'.

My seventeen-year-old son showed wisdom beyond his years when he said,

'Mum, you should follow your dream. Life is too short to miss an opportunity. Look at Paul Landa, forty-three, playing tennis, and he just dropped dead. At least try and see if it is possible and then try to make it happen'.

So I did. Carly, the owner, had not wanted to sell to a man who rode the mare too roughly, to a couple that just wanted a brood mare, or to a prospective endurance rider. She was happy with her father's report of me, and she even agreed to let me pay by instalment when she heard the story of my birthday treat and my lack of finance. The following summer, when Chianti competed in her first dressage test, Carly and her husband were there with a baby in a stroller.

The summer that Chianti came into our lives is one I will never forget. I may have taught my son to drive, but he taught me a more valuable lesson about perseverance and following your dream.

CHAPTER 42

1985 – Not a Good Year

THE EARLY DAYS WITH Chianti was quite a test for Michael and I. She was virtually a country horse, or rather she had not set hoof outside the Bringelly property. Now she was in the Sydney suburb of Belrose, and although there was a large bushland adjoining the riding school, there was likely to be the odd track clearing equipment, left by the firefighting crew, to cause sudden terror. She had been the only baby at home; now she was surrounded by thirty riding school horses, including a stallion who made improper suggestions to her as he came down the lane. I was so concerned with her behaviour, I asked a visiting vet if I could do anything to help her.

'Of course, she's an Arab, that is a very flighty breed. You could try giving her a vitamin B shot to settle her nerves' was his advice, and that did prove to be helpful. Also, regular work, taking out the trail rides, improved her attitude, but not before I had been dumped out on the track twice when something untoward startled her into spinning violently and galloping home riderless. Not a good look at a riding school, where anxious parents stand around waiting for their darlings to return. Michael was anxious to show her off, so come January, we decided to try a gymkhana at St Ives showground. When I tried to exercise her in the ring, she panicked and reared so high, I just slid off her back. When Michael rode her in his riding class, he let her get too close to the horse next to her, and she kicked out at it. We thought she had better have some serious training before we went again. Jacqui, a friend from Seaforth days, offered to give Michael some coaching, so that was arranged for every second Saturday.

January 1985 was when Michael found a new girlfriend, Eve. She was not a schoolgirl. She was working in the city but living with her parents in the western suburbs.

'Eve is the real thing', Michael told me. 'I really love her, and yes, I am using protection'.

Do you really find your soulmate at seventeen? Well, my sister Margaret found her Joe at fifteen, rapidly producing Paul and Debbie, and they were together for fifty years until death did them part.

Michael and Eve made a beautiful couple, and I was happy that they seemed to be so happy together.

In retrospect, 1985 was not a good year. Firstly, Reg and his girlfriend had already moved to Gunnedah, so there was no more losing Greg for the weekend. Then, sometime early in the year, Matthew and his girlfriend set sail for the UK, so Michael lost his lodgings. Phillip had an accident on a quad bike and damaged his back, so Michael moved in with Phillip so that he could still attend Grammar and look after Phillip. Eve would also frequently stay there. Greg was faced with coming to the riding school with me or staying with his football mate, who had the horse-mad sister. I continued with working two jobs and coping with two geographically opposite sons. I certainly did not have any time for any romantic association.

Things took a turn for the worse one Friday when Michael rang me to say that he could not make his horse-riding session with Jacqui the following day as he and Eve had something special planned. He would ring me Saturday night instead. As I couldn't contact Jacqui, I let the horse-mad girl from Avalon have the training ride on Chianti. That night, the phone call from Michael was a definite worry.

'Mum, I am at the hospital. We have had an accident, and Eve has a broken leg. I will call you tomorrow', and he hung up before I could ask which hospital. Remember, this was in the pre–mobile phone days.

What to do? I wanted to run and be with my boy, but where was he? I didn't even know Eve's last name. First, I rang Phillip to see if Michael was there and whether he knew Eve's last name. Phillip was just as vague as I was but promised to ring me when Michael turned up. So I started ringing hospitals, but none would answer my questions when I didn't have the patient's name.

It was the following morning before I had a phone call from Phillip to say Michael was there, so I made a quick call to the riding school to absent myself for the day and drove into town. Michael was obviously the worse for wear. The smell of alcohol was pervasive, and it took a long time for him to become coherent. The story was an unfortunate repeat of my happier birthday experience. When Mathew left Sydney, he left behind his driver's licence, and as he was also a tanned, blond-headed youth, Michael had used it as his. He and Eve had looked at a motorbike for sale, had taken it for a spin and made a snappy right-hand turn, but not snappy enough, and they had been collected by a car. Eve had broken her leg and been taken to the hospital. Michael had shown his false licence to the police and gone to the hospital with Eve and finished the night getting drunk with a mate. This mate had gear that would take the pain away, and that was when Michael had his first taste of heroin.

That last information I would not receive that day, only later when his addiction became more evident. Phillip called a lawyer friend to sort out Michael's problem with the law, and motorbikes became a taboo subject. That was also the end of Michael's commitment to improving his horse riding.

The year 1985 was Michael's HSC year, and I was anxious to help him achieve the marks he needed to get into university. He had chosen to do 3U French, English and modern history; 2U economics; and 1U general studies. Phillip would help with French and economics, and I could do English, history and general studies.

I checked the English texts and looked for planned performances and then looked at the modern history and general studies syllabuses. I tried to convince Michael that he needed to spend one day of the weekend going over his studies, but here I met failure. He was confident he could cover his subjects during Monday to Friday and spend the weekend with Eve. He did agree to go to see the plays on the English syllabus on a Saturday.

There was no way that I could keep control of Michael's movements. He would tell me he was keeping up to date with assignments and sometimes ring and ask help with an essay, but I just had to rely on the belief that he wanted to go to university and knew he had to achieve the mark to get there.

It wasn't until just before Michael's eighteenth birthday that Phillip told me he had proof that Michael was regularly using heroin. I could not believe my ears! How could my beautiful son, who had been so proud of his body and whose nickname had once been Veg as he tried being a vegetarian, be abusing his body with such a deadly drug. When I confronted him with my amazement that he could do this, his reply was many creative and brilliant people found heroin stimulating, and if you knew how to handle it, you were okay. I realised he was actually on a heroin high when he said that, as at a later stage, he told me the dark side of being controlled by the drug and how it took away all the good things in life.

So heroin was still in control when he went to the year 6 formal with Eve and sat for the HSC exam. All the places I called for help explained that until the addict sought help, there was little I could do. As soon as the exams were over, Michael agreed to try to abstain, and Phillip organised drugs from the local GP to see him through a cold turkey withdrawal in Bali for a month.

Michael was not due to return until 2 January 1986, when I was going to go with him and Greg to Phillip's farm near Kempsey.

However, he returned on 30 December 1985, which, unbeknownst to me, was the anniversary of his meeting Eve. He went straight from the airport to the Exchange Hotel, where they had met, but Eve was not there. Michael met another girl he knew there, and they came back to Phillip's apartment block and, in the swimming pool area, shared heroin again. The pool attendant found Michael dead there on the morning of 31 December 1985.

CHAPTER 43

1986 — Flight to Carroll

I DROVE HOME THAT morning, still numb from identifying my son's beautiful body. I had tickets for Greg and I to fly to Tamworth to tell Reg. This was something that had to be done in person, not by telephone. Greg was excited about going with his mate's parents to see the New Year fireworks at Newport Hotel, so I did not tell him the awful news. What could one day later matter? What I did tell him was that we were going to fly to Tamworth to see his dad on New Year's Day. That afternoon, I tried ringing funeral parlours. I had rung three before I found the type of voice I could talk to. I simply could not ring anyone else, not my mother, Reg's girls or my closest friends. I felt I just wanted to find a hole and bury myself with my son. But of course, there was the living son to consider and protect. Staying awake to welcome him home early on New Year's Day, I warned him we would have to leave fairly early for the airport.

A quick breakfast and then I broke the terrible news. We were going to see Reg to tell him Michael had died from a drug overdose. Shock, disbelief and then horror flashed across Greg's face, and after the immediate questions of when, how and why were hurled at me, he immediately phoned his mate to tell him his brother had 'karked it' and we were going to tell his dad. I thought how different we were; I couldn't bear to tell anyone, and Greg was about to tell everyone as he started a second phone call.

Once at the airport, Greg found an eatery and stocked up on sweet things. My throat was so closed, I couldn't drink, let alone eat.

At Tamworth airport, I took the rented car and drove to Carroll, a little hamlet halfway between Tamworth and Gunnedah, where Reg lived with Sharon. Unfortunately, they were not home, and the next-door neighbour thought they had gone to Sydney for New

Year. There was a working public phone outside the general store at Carroll, so I rang Karen to see if Reg had stayed with her. Yes was the answer, but he was returning home today. So I drove to Keepit Dam, a quiet, relaxing place with picnickers and children swimming, and Greg and I had a long talk about Michael's life and mistakes. We both cried and hugged and felt prepared to visit Reg.

By the time we returned to Reg's place, the motorbike was in the driveway; the travellers had returned. To say Reg was surprised to see me would be an understatement, and by the look of our tear-stained faces, he knew the news would not be good. However, he was totally unprepared for the finality of what had happened, and for the second time that day, I was shattered by the pain and anguish seared across the face of someone I had loved. In a similar reaction to Greg, Reg was immediately on the phone to his mother and to his girls, giving the sad news so abruptly, I flinched. That evening, I slept in their spare bed, haunted by the sound of sobbing.

It was an obvious choice for Greg to stay with Reg and return with him for the funeral, so with a heavy heart, I drove back to Tamworth and flew home.

Now I had to organise a funeral, and once again, I had to have my mother told in person, not by telephone, so I asked Joe, my brother-in-law, to tell my sister if they could drive to Forster and tell my mother. This they did, but my sister decided to visit my mother's doctor first to see if he thought she could stand the shock.

'As long as she is surrounded by love, she will be okay, and if she needs to be by her daughter's side at the funeral, she should go' were his wise words, so my mother did make the trip and sat next to me.

Karen had been confused by Reg's phone call, wondering whether he was hallucinating, but then she remembered my strange phone call and was anxious to contact me. All three girls, plus Reg's mum and dad and our closest friends from Seaforth days, came to the funeral. Some wanted to see the body, which the funeral people organised; however, I don't remember whether they had asked for clothes, but I certainly did not supply any, and Michael had been skinny-dipping, so his body was naked. The unfortunate result was that those close relatives who viewed the body saw only a head appearing from swaddling! I worked for days on the eulogy, trying to keep it under twenty minutes, which the funeral arranger said was the absolute maximum. I was determined to read it myself and to try and do justice to my son's eventful short life.

Early on the morning of the funeral, Michael's one-time girlfriend, Michelle, arrived at my place, carrying a huge wreath. We went to Whale Beach, where she and Michael had been many times, and we strolled along the wet sand, talking about old times. Barbara, Phillip's secretary, drove us to the funeral, and mourners filled the room. I was somewhat taken aback when I recognised one of the pall-bearers as being an ex-student of Narrabeen High. Reg was there with Greg, who said he was happy to come home with me. Back at my home in Avalon, Barbara had organised food, and Eve met Reg, who was quite disappointed she wasn't pregnant and therefore of little use. An unexpected arrival was my good friend Ann, now married, with her two children, Patrick and Nada. Ann had woken with a strong feeling she should see me, so she came all the way from Bondi Junction.

Amongst the cards of condolence was one from Marg, Reg's first wife, which read,

'I can only imagine the pain of losing a child. Please remember my girls are your girls also. They will always be there for you'.

To this very day, they always have been.

The first family occasion in January 1986 was the wedding of Vicki, Reg's middle daughter, to Peter. This was held at Spinks Park in Lismore, with the reception at Lismore Town Hall. Greg and I travelled by train, and at the reception, when various people were giving speeches to the happy couple, Greg told me he would have liked to say his brother Michael would have loved to be there and see Vicki looking so beautiful. I persuaded him that we shouldn't enter a sad thought on such a happy day, but he or I could tell her before we left the following day. I don't know if we ever did, but I realised just how much he missed his brother, who had always been there.

Vicki's union with Peter was long-lasting, producing three beautiful daughters, Caitlyn, Sophie and Adrienne.

In the following weeks, Greg's friends were very supportive of him, coming around, taking off on bike rides, going to the movies and the beach. I was grateful to their parents as I thought they may not want their children to be associated with the brother of a drug-overdose victim, but Greg had held these friendships for over six years, so the bonds were strong.

I, on the other hand, self-isolated from friends, refusing offers to come and stay or go out. John Morgan was quick to ring me when he heard the news, but I refused his offer of comforting talk; my divorce papers insisted both boys should not be brought into contact with him. So it was a very lonely soul-searching time for me. Amazing how you can be lonely in a house full of people as Greg had asked me if a friend of his could stay in Michael's room. This was Richard, whose parents had recently split, his mother living with her new partner in Umina and his dad living in Manly. Richard moved in and then was joined by his brother, Tim, who brought his own swag and slept on the floor. Both boys had casual jobs as kitchen assistants at a restaurant in Avalon, so they were able to pay a little rent, but both were older than Greg and had already started drinking and smoking, although not in my house.

At the end of term 1, Narrabeen High School had a parent–teacher evening that was held in the school library, so I was expected to attend. It just happened that both Richard and Tim were working that night, so I asked Greg if he would mind spending the evening with his friend who lived down the street and then checked with the parents to see if that would be okay. I arrived home to an empty house and was just enjoying the peace and quiet when a knock on the door announced the arrival of the police! They told me my son had been found breaking into a school and was being held at the police station! They checked my licence and said that I'd better drive down to pick him up.

Never in my wildest dreams would I have thought this could happen. Not as part of a gang out to destroy, just a lonely little boy who broke a window and stole a smiley stamp. Greg looked very sheepish and embarrassed, and the smell of alcohol was obvious. Apparently, he had an argument with his mate and had come home, drunk the remnants of the wine from the wake, then ridden his bike to Avalon Primary School, broken a window to get in and walked the corridor, switching on the lights as he went, finally reaching his previous sixth-grade classroom and stealing a smiley stamp from the desk. I signed a release form, which bound me to take Greg to the children's court on a date to be advised.

Back at home, Greg had no explanation for his actions; he just sobbed in my arms and asked, 'Will I be sent away?'

'No, you are definitely a first offender. You were obviously emotionally upset and grieving, and we will fight this. But you have to show that you are a responsible person, not a thief'.

This news was bad but okay to impart by telephone, so I rang Reg the following day. He told me to let him know when the case would be heard, and he would come to Sydney to attend.

Both Richard and Tim were concerned about Greg and convinced the owner of the restaurant Tim worked at to give Greg a part-time job as a kitchen hand, so Greg's Saturdays were filled, off to the riding school with me at 8am, home for tea, and then I would drive him to work at 7pm and pick him up at 10pm. Greg proved to be a good worker, and the money he earned was attractive. He started talking about quitting school and becoming a full-time employee.

Sometime in August, Greg's court appearance was scheduled at Glebe Children's Court, and Reg, Greg and I arrived early to meet with the duty solicitor. I came prepared with a detailed account of Greg's and Michael's attendance at Avalon Primary School and the winning of the BMX bike. Then Michael's unexpected death on 31 December and Greg's consumption of the remnants of the wake before going to the school. There was also a reference from the owner of the restaurant, stating Greg's good work record.

Reg spoke to the solicitor, and then after I had given evidence, the solicitor asked Reg to speak. Reg then told the judge he was willing to take Greg away from the drug scene at Avalon to the peaceful country village of Carroll, where he could go to school or get a job.

The eventual finding was that Greg was found guilty but, under some legal clause, would not have the charge recorded against him as there were sufficient mitigating circumstances. Then the court recommended that he live with his father in Carroll.

So Greg was sent away after all, but he was happy with that arrangement, happy to forget schooling and education and get a paying job at Gunnedah abattoir.

I felt I was the one punished, having lost one son, and I was to be prevented from keeping the second. I could not bear to stay in the house with Richard and Tim, so I moved into a small bedsit in Mona Vale. Eventually, both boys moved out, and I had a lovely couple with two boys, a baby girl and a fox terrier dog renting, until the death of a parent enabled them to buy the house I could never return to.

But 1986 did have two positive outcomes for me. In August of that year, Val Morgan had a heart operation, which she did not survive. John Morgan was able to come and visit and resume our comforting conversations. In 1988, having lost his wife, his mother and his best friend within two years, John had a heart attack, followed by a triple bypass. On his release from the hospital, I moved in to take care of him, even though his son, Bruce, was already living there, as I did not trust Bruce's smoking or dietary habits.

In November 1986, I exhibited Chianti as Brujanie Park Yarah, her registered name, in the National Arabian Stud Horse Show held in the Sydney Showgrounds. We competed in the Novice Part-Bred Arabian Mare under saddle, and in a class of twenty-seven, we were called in and eventually placed seventh. Unfortunately, only six ribbons were awarded, but I was still elated at the result, and John was there, videoing the whole event.

That was the year I decided to leave Narrabeen High and try a new environment. I mentioned this to an English teacher on the staff, who had been a school librarian previously, and we decided to offer the department a joint application. I would apply for a transfer in the Northern Beaches area, and she would apply for my vacated position as school librarian. Apparently, this was not considered to be correct procedure, and both of our carefully worded submissions were sent to our headmaster, who was not pleased. My compatriot immediately resigned, and I tore up my transfer request. Late that year, I received a transfer to Manly High School.

CHAPTER 44

1987 – Greg in Carroll

GREG MADE NO EFFORT to finish his schooling but quickly found a job at the abattoirs and rode his bike to work. He also made quite an impression on the girls of Carroll. I made a trip to see him, and he tried to introduce me to his new girlfriend, Nancye Riley, but she was too shy to meet me. Later that year, Greg told me Nancye was pregnant and did not want an abortion. He said he had told her, 'Well, I guess I will have to marry you'.

But Nancye was too strong in nature to accept this half-hearted proposal and said she would manage on her own. How difficult that would have been for her, still living at home, being one of seven children, where none of the others had encountered such shame.

On 4 September 1987, Nancye's little girl, Stephanie Michelle, my granddaughter, was born. Greg had nothing to do with his offspring as he felt, being still sixteen, he was too young to be a father, but not too young to have impregnated the mother, so I thought I should support Nancye on his behalf.

Greg was now seeing another girl in Carroll, Leeanne, and very soon, she too was pregnant. On 28 August 1989, my grandson, Michael Gregory Mahoney, was born. Reg had separated from Sharon and was living in a different house in Carroll, and Greg and Leeanne had moved in with him. This time, Greg was much happier about being a father. The Cappers had accepted him and treated him as a son. Reg was happy to be a grandfather to a baby boy, and Leeanne was a doting mother. However, the strain of new parenthood was too much for the couple, and within a couple of years, Leeanne got out. Greg was heartbroken when she found another partner.

So now I had two grandchildren living in the same country area and, to my knowledge, unknowing about their blood relationship.

The two mothers had never been friends or even associates, even though both lived in the tiny hamlet of Carroll. The age difference of six years meant that they moved in different friendship circles. I felt compelled to bring my two grandchildren together to make sure they realised they were brother and sister. So with the cooperation of John Morgan with his four-wheel drive and caravan, I made a yearly visit to Carroll to see each grandchild, separately at first and then together. These were lovely times for me. I can clearly remember visiting Mrs Riley and watching three-year-old Stephanie performing a repertoire of songs and dances and then visiting the Cappers and watching one-year-old Michael just walking, with a huge smile, an absolute image of his dad at the same age.

In December 1990, John and I celebrated Greg's twentieth birthday by taking Stephanie swimming at the river, and we had birthday cake in the car as the day was too windy to light candles outside. The autumn of following year, we took Greg, Leeanne and Michael to visit both grandparents, my mother in Forster and Reg's parents in Port Macquarie. Then both girls moved to Gunnedah, Nancy living with Shane and Leeanne living with Rod.

Back in 1988, Brisbane hosted an expo, and John and I decided to go, travelling via Gunnedah, in case Greg wanted to come, but he didn't. In Brisbane, we stayed with Sandra, who was living with her partner, Franc. One night, we minded their toddler, Brenton, who was less than one year old. When I finished in the kitchen, about 6.30pm, I couldn't find Brenton. How can a less-than-one-year-old disappear in such a short time? Mouth dry, chest constricted with fear, heart pumping alarmingly, I finally looked into the master's bedroom, whose door had been left open. There was Brenton, curled up in his cot, fast asleep! The side of the cot had been left down, so he had obviously climbed in because he was tired! What a perfect baby to mind!

CHAPTER 45

1988 — A New Passion

AFTER JOHN HAD HIS triple bypass in 1988, I moved in to his home in Manly Vale to look after him, but as he grew stronger, so did our attraction, and soon we were sharing the double bed. One evening, he took me to the Manly Civic Club for dinner, and as we sat enjoying our coffee, a young girl began setting up an amplifier and speaker and announced she was about to do a line dancing session, if anyone wanted to join in. Any type of dancing will attract me, from tap and ballet as a preschooler to ballroom as a teenager, so I was happy to become involved. After watching for a little while, John disappeared to play the pokies, and I stayed for the two-hour session. The following week, I returned alone and, from there, heard about Lindsay and his wife teaching at the other club in Manly. This led to dancing with Rosalie at Frenchs Forest, Julie Talbot at Seaforth and Willoughby and Vicki at Brookvale. With friends made at these classes, I danced at the Sydney Royal Easter Show, both the old venue and the new Homebush arena, scoring free entry tickets each time. Then I was invited to join a group going to the Tamworth Country Music Festival, where my snoring forced my roommate, a lovely Dutch lady, to move her mattress to the floor of the second bedroom to be able to get some sleep. After that first night, I would not go to bed until I heard her breathing, indicating she was already asleep. The problem with my snoring, of which John never complained, was only resolved in 2007 when, following recurrent high blood pressure readings, my doctor referred me to a sleep specialist, who diagnosed sleep apnoea. From that day on, I have slept with a CPAP machine, enabling me to share a room with a travelling companion without inconveniencing them. Apart from that problem, it was a wonderful four days, dancing and partying. Even though the temperature out west in January can be daunting, I would urge all line dancers to at least go once.

Finally, Vicki, who taught line dancing at Brookvale Primary School Hall, decided to enter a novice team in the Annual Line Dancing Competition held at St Marys. That opened a whole new aspect of line dance. Steps had to be perfectly executed, and timing was essential so that a team of six would turn as one. Just one dance but perfected over weeks, then dressed in matching costumes, we finally performed, coming second!

I continued with line dancing, finally joining the Manly Senior Centre group, and when the teacher there retired, I took up teaching, first with Marcelle and then with Yvonne and Ruby, continuing to do so into my eighties.

CHAPTER 46

1990 – Chianti Becomes a Mother

I WAS STILL COMPELLED to work two jobs to pay the mortgage, plus Chianti's upkeep, but without Greg at home, I was able to spend more time training Chianti. First, I tried to get her relaxed with lots of walking on a loose rein, changing directions, cantering on either leading leg, square halt and rein back. When she seemed happy and relaxed, and after several trips to Frenchs Forest Showground, we tried, successfully to have her registered as an Australian stock horse, although she had never met a cow in her life and probably would have run away in fright if she had. Then I joined Northside Riding Club and competed in novice dressage competitions, managing to come third, and received a yellow rosette. This, together with a blue first ribbon in led mare over fifteen hands, completed our showing trophies, although I still counted our near miss of a ribbon at the national. By now, Chianti was eight years old, and I felt it was time for her to become a mother.

Unfortunately, Gunner, the Arabian stallion, had passed away, but his replacement, Madrid, was a beautiful Andalusian, whose father had been in the El Caballo Blanco team in Melbourne. I was able to introduce them on a fairly regular basis, until the time was right and the mating was completed easily.

Now I had to plan for as natural a birth as possible, but one where I hopefully could take a part. I had tried turning Chianti into a natural grass-eating horse by taking her and Greg to Phillip's farm in Yarrahapinni. No such luck. She ate grass intermittently but would wait at the gate to be fed and wouldn't get her feet wet walking into the dam to drink water; she was so used to a trough! I was getting quite desperate when one of the girls at the riding school recommended a place that had cows and horses and was run by an ex-nursing sister, who would ring the vet if an animal seemed unwell. Just what I wanted. So I made the trip to Box Hill and met Joy, who welcomed Chianti with open arms, saying,

'That is perfect as we have a mare due about the same time and they will be good company for each other'.

She showed me the foaling paddock, which was right in front of the house, and then said,

'I do hope you will be able to come and stay when she is due as I feel a maiden mare needs constant watching. The vet has given me a warning halter to wake me up when she goes down, but I wouldn't get any sleep any way, so I would want you to take the night shift from that bedroom overlooking the paddock'.

What wonderful news, I had been considering asking if I could set up a tent nearby.

As luck would have it, Chianti was due early October, right in the school holidays, so everything was wonderful. Chianti moved in, nibbled grass, but was still hard fed, and her water was in a trough. She and the bay mare seemed to get on well, and both blossomed and grew fat. I stopped riding her, just happy to brush and spoil her, thrilled at the way she would come when I called. Preparation for this baby was a balm to my soul, scarred by the loss of one and the removal of my other son.

As September approached, I grew anxious about whether Chianti would come earlier than expected; she was so large.

Luckily, she was still holding when school holidays arrived, and I moved into Joy's house in Box Hill. Three nights, nothing to report, but the following night, both mares were very active, walking the fence line, one behind the other. Suddenly, the alarm halter sounded, and I rushed outside to see Chianti on the ground, right in front of the main door. I could hear her panting, almost groaning, and I realised what every prospective father must feel when they watch their partner give birth. There is the one you love in pain and distress, and you are the one who has caused that distress.

Suddenly, the sounds paused, and Chianti stood up and started to sniff the grass, but I could see there was a large black shape protruding from her rear, a foal still in its birth sack, not quite ready to be born! I could see the outline of the foal quite clearly now, and to my horror, it seemed to be hind legs and bum protruding. I ran to tell Simone, Joy's daughter, who had just appeared with a phone in her hand to ring the vet. How do you tell a maiden mare that it really isn't over yet and she has to finish the job!

Nature really is amazing. The next moment, there was a sucking sound, and that black bundle disappeared back into her innards. Then she lay down again, more noise, and out came the foal in its bag, right side up, with head and front legs pointing down. Simone was able to tell the vet everything was okay and he could come at a more respectable time. Chianti was standing over her foal, licking off the covering, while we stood back and let her do what comes naturally. Then the foal struggled to stand, fell over and tried again, and it finally stood, leaning on his mother. I did not touch either of them, just gazed at the scene I felt so privileged to have watched.

When the vet arrived the following morning, he reported the mother and son were healthy and then said,

'You will have a fine-looking grey there'.

I was astounded as I was looking at a definitely brown foal with two back white socks and a white star on his forehead. This was when I learned that white horses are not born white; nature camouflages them in a protective brown coat, which will change from brown to red dapple, then blue dapple, steely grey and finally white in old age. The telltale signs that Sangria would become a grey were the sprinkling of grey hairs above his eyes. I watched him change colour through his early years until he reached dappled grey, still with the black mane, tail and legs and white back socks, although the star had disappeared.

CHAPTER 47

1991 — Greg in Trouble

IN 1991, GREG WAS in trouble with the law again, stealing cigarettes and being drunk and in possession of marijuana. He rang me to say he had to go to court and asked if I could come and bail him out of some debt he owed. I travelled to Carroll, and Greg and I stayed with the Cappers. This time, the court also found him guilty and issued a fine and a period of probation, during which time he was to return to live with me and John.

I don't think John was enamoured by this prospect, but the true friend that he was, he made no objection. Because both John and I had given up smoking back in 1988 when John had a bypass, there was absolutely no smoking in the house in Manly Vale. Because neither John nor I drank alcohol and Greg seemed to have a problem with it, no alcohol was to be consumed at home. Finally, if Greg happened to meet a girl he fancied, he was to bring her home to meet us before he took her to bed. I said I did not want to stumble across an unknown female on my way to the bathroom in the middle of the night. Greg accepted these rules and tried to keep them. He needed a job, but the few positions Centrelink offered did not work out. Eventually, Paul offered to train him as a plasterer, but that lasted only a few weeks before Greg injured himself and so was off work on compo. I think Greg was rather depressed at this stage. He had been ringing the Cappers, hoping to contact Leeanne, and I found him in tears, saying that Leeanne didn't want to be with him anymore.

My fiftieth birthday was on 18 November 1991, and I celebrated by going to El Caballo Blanco with John, Greg and my close friends. It was a wonderful day, and Brenda took the nicest photo of Greg and me.

Greg's twenty-first birthday was on 3 December 1991, which we celebrated going to Refuge Bay on Paul's yacht. Paul, Karen and five-year-old Jesse and two-year-old Matt, sister Sandi, cousin Debbie, two friends from Avalon days and Lindy, a friend of Paul who gave everyone wave board rides, towed behind her runabout.

Lovely, happy times, then Christmas and the New Year, completely unknowing what the new year would bring. At first, the year was good. Cousin Debbie had a twenty-first birthday party, which we attended and which Greg did not want to leave as he had made another conquest with one of Debbie's friends, but Penrith seemed geographically impossible to continue the relationship.

Greg was not really happy living in Manly Vale. He didn't have a job, and the friends he had maintained from Seaforth days were all employed, so he was at a loose end during the day. He didn't have a car or even a bike to get around and became depressed trying to find a job. I suggested he tried going to TAFE to improve his career possibilities, but he had missed so much schooling that he wasn't prepared to try again. Then one Thursday night, he went to Manly with a mate and came home very late. I had been unable to get to sleep, so I heard him arrive and a distinctive girlish giggle. I was annoyed that he had broken our agreement and had obviously brought a girl home, so I went to confront them. There was a very happy Greg holding a tiny scrap of a girl in his arms, snuggling into bed.

We had a brief altercation, I reminding him of the promise he had made and he telling me that this girl, Karina, lived in the city and the Manly ferry run had finished for the night and they did not have enough money to get a taxi. What could I do? Certainly not throw them out, just reiterate my displeasure. The following day, on my way to school, I dropped them both off at Brookvale, where Greg had to report to his parole officer.

That afternoon, Greg said he was about to move in with the new girlfriend and asked if I could drive them into town. I said I would the following day and then talked to him about being careful in the city and not getting drunk or trying drugs. At the last suggestion, he laughed and said,

'You can trust me, Mum. I won't stuff up, promise!'

The following day, 15 May, was John's birthday. I had invited John's daughter Lee; her husband, Graeme; and children, Tim, aged eight, and Chris, aged five, to dinner, but first I drove to Burke St, Woolloomooloo, so that I would know where this girl and my son would be staying and then back home to prepare dinner. We were still seated at the table, chatting, when a knock at the door announced two policemen had arrived. Lee, Graeme and the children immediately disappeared upstairs as the police proceeded to tell me my son had been found dead in the Burke St unit I had left him. How could this have happened? How could lightning strike twice and take both my sons?

The police told me I needed to go to the Glebe coroner's unit and identify the body, so Graeme took his sons home, and John, Lee and I drove into town. So peaceful did Greg look, as if he had gone to sleep and not woken up, which was exactly what had happened. I don't think I cried; I was totally in shock. The tears would come later. Now I had to face the necessity of telling his father that both of his longed-for sons had perished under my watch.

Once again, it needed to be a visit, not a phone call, so the following day, John and I set off for Wauchope, where Reg was living with his new girlfriend. John felt Reg would not want to see him with me, so he decided to play golf in Taree while I drove there alone. This time, Reg almost anticipated the bad news when he saw me. Then shock, horror, disbelief and unbearable grief flashed across his face.

'Have we been so bad to deserve this?' he gasped.

I was so relieved that he had said 'we'. If there was going to be blame, then we would share it. Once again, we cried in each other's arms, while the new girlfriend kept a discrete distance.

Finally, it was time to collect John from golf, so ensuring Reg I would give him details of the funeral I was yet to organise, I drove back to the clubhouse. The following day, a Sunday, I stayed in bed. I had slept in the spare room where Greg had slept, and as I hadn't changed the sheets, I felt I could still smell my son and obviously the girl he had had sex with two nights before. Writing this now, that seems revolting, but at the time, it was necessary. I really had the need to hold on to any remains of Greg I could salvage. Later, when I visited the Burke St apartment to collect his things, I was able to sleep with a T-shirt he had worn for a few nights.

John was such a wonderful support. He visited Manly High School Monday morning instead of just telephoning to say I was unwell. He told the deputy the whole story and how he was going to take me away for a month and asked if they could organise a long service leave to cover this time.

Once again, I rang the same funeral people, arranged for Greg's best clothes to be worn and planned my brother-in-law to tell my mother. Reg told his mother and daughters, and John told our best friends. This time, I had no way of keeping people away.

Brenda, a long-standing friend, came to sit with me while I made the necessary phone calls and helped me through the panic attack that ensued. This time, I had a contingent from Carroll, Greg, Kath and Leeanne Capper with little Michael and Nancye, with a new boyfriend Shane, but without Stephanie. To keep the two girls apart, I rang my friend Pam from the riding school, who took the Cappers off to visit some nurseries. Fortunately, John's house had plenty of room. So the Cappers had the spare bedroom, the Rileys slept on the upstairs lounge, my mother slept on the downstairs lounge as she couldn't manage the stairs, and my brother, Ian, who had driven Mum down and would take her back home, slept in the caravan. Once again, I struggled to fit Greg's life into a twenty-minute eulogy, which I managed to read the following day. Pam introduced Reg to his grandson, Michael, whom he had not seen for two years.

The following Monday, I went to see the girl who had been with Greg when he died. She was in the hospital, and the staff were a little concerned that I wanted to see her, thinking I might attack her, I suppose. All I wanted was her account of Greg's last night. Was he happy or depressed? Was he looking forward to life with her or ready to end it all? These were the questions only Karina could answer, and she did. Yes, Greg was happy; they had just had more wonderful sex. She needed her heroin fix, and he decided to try. He had another beer and went to sleep and did not wake up. End of story, nothing more to say. He had died with the health department's warning pamphlet about the dangers of mixing heroin and alcohol there on the table.

The following week, I was on a plane to Fiji. I was totally numb, unfeeling, going through the motions of waking, nibbling at food, traveling and fitfully sleeping, barely alive. John was always by my side, comforting and encouraging me, urging me forward. Without him, I think I would have just curled up and died; life was not worth living anymore. Back home, John's first trip was to Blackmores to buy copious amounts of vitamins that he had been assured would aid my recovery and bring new vitality. Dutifully I swallowed handfuls, not in the least convinced they would do any good, but simply to avoid wasting the expense. I had to go and ride Chianti, and the lonely trail rides were probably good for my soul, crying long heartrending sobs until I could cry no more, washing my face in the creek and galloping back home, berating myself for being so weak. I really thought the pain would never end, but little by little, I was able to get myself out of bed before lunchtime, struggle to the shops and cook a meal, even if I couldn't face eating it. Then the month was over, and I was back at school. Nobody mentioned the reason for my absence; they just welcomed me back as I settled into the familiar routine.

Suddenly, it seemed as if there were not enough to do to keep my mind in work mode, so I decided to launch into the Gifted and Talented Programme I had looked at previously. I offered to take all year 7 classes one period a week as I had done in term 1 to hone their library skills, but this time, they would do future problem-solving. By the second year, a group of four who wanted to continue the programme won their way to the Australian championships held in

Melbourne. There they won the badge design competition and came third overall but missed out on a trip to the USA, which the school probably would not have been able to fund.

Two things I decided to do were to become an Australian citizen and to change my name from Mahoney to my birth name of Wood. I had no need to keep my married name as both children of that name were now gone. By reverting to my birth name of Wood, I could wipe out all trace of my adopted name of Vinnard and married name Mahoney. I felt reborn as an Australian, as strong and resilient as the name I bore.

CHAPTER 48

1993 – Indonesia

CHRISTMAS 1992, I SPENT in Forster, but from then on, I decided I would never again spend that time of year in Australia. Each Xmas holiday, I hoped to travel overseas and spend the year planning and saving towards that goal. John was very happy to go along with this plan, and our first trip together was to Indonesia. John had been there before with Val, and he wanted to show me what had impressed him. I bought a copy of Lonely Planet's Guide to Indonesia and found things I wanted to see, so our trip was a combination of both. We spent most of the time in Java, traveling by bus, riding horses up Mt Bromo to see the sun rise over the volcano, watching the Wayun Kulit or shadow puppet theatre, listening to the gamelan orchestra in Jakarta and marvelling at the carvings of Borobudur. Once we were inadvertently on the wrong bus as I was still practising my Indonesian language and my pronunciation wasn't very good. When I realised we were going in the wrong direction, going north instead of west to the coastal town of Pacitan, we rushed to explain to the driver, with several other passengers with varying amounts of English trying to sort out our problem. Once the driver understood the situation, he kindly made a short detour to connect us to the right bus, firstly announcing in rapid Indonesian to his passengers what he was about to do. This was met with laughter and smiles from all. I pondered on how such a situation would have been met in my hometown of Sydney.

But our most exciting bus trip was between Jakarta and Bandung when we were finally out on a country single-lane highway, away from the city's streets, and met an impressive traffic jam, cars at a standstill as far as the eye could see, stationary, going up a hill. Our bus driver did not pause but immediately moved into the oncoming lane, which fortunately was empty, and continued up the hill, overtaking everyone. When a car appeared in this lane, he moved the bus to the side gravel of the oncoming traffic lane, still moving at a moderate speed, and was finally stopped by a roadside stall directly in front. Now, I thought, we would be here forever as the traffic in our correct lane was creeping forward and a steady stream of cars was continuing in the opposite lane. Suddenly, out of our bus jumped the man from the front seat, all smiles and waves as he stopped the oncoming traffic. Little by little, our bus moved across in front of an increasing line of cars and into our correct lane. All done with smiles, waves and such calm cheerfulness, I was absolutely astounded. I thought maybe the buses here are kings of the road and mere car and truck drivers pay them respect. Once again, I pondered at what a similar scene would have been like in Sydney.

We spent the final week in Bali, which was rather a culture shock after the polite people of Java, meeting heaps of loud-mouthed, drunken Aussies. In Java, I had heard someone say,

'Bali is not Indonesia. It is another state of Australia!'

When the Bali bombing attack happened in 2002, I was not surprised that the fanatical Muslim group, who abhorred drinking alcohol, had selected Paddy's Pub, a favourite hangout of large crowds of inebriated Australians. I also remembered reading about the other target, the Sari Club, in my Lonely Planet guidebook. Apparently, Indonesians had to pay the equivalent of a standard weekly wage to gain entry, so very few attended.

CHAPTER 49

1994 – Malaysia

CIRCUMSTANCES CAN SEEM EERILY strange at times. In 1992, my son, Greg, had died on my partner John's birthday. In 1994, my mother awoke on her birthday, 23 August, to find her husband, Sidney, dead beside her from a sudden heart attack. Over the phone, she had gasped out the news to me, and immediately, John and I were on our way to Forster. All six children arrived as I organised the funeral, my third, so I felt quite competent. My brother, Ian, who had been living and working in Newcastle said he would take a redundancy package and move back home to look after Mum and Owen. I was relieved as I had thought I would be expected to move to Forster as I had no dependents and a job that would enable me to transfer into the area. It turned out to be a good move for Ian as in Forster he met Kirsty, and they were a couple by the year 2001 and married in 2004.

In 1993, I took my mum on my annual trip to Gunnedah so she could meet her great-granddaughter, Stephanie, who by this time had a baby brother, Jacob, and a dad, Shane, and then on to meet her great-grandson, Michael, who had a brother, Brandon, and a dad, Rod.

It was then that the family secret was revealed. Nancye had told Stephanie that Michael was her brother, but Michael had no knowledge of this fact, until one day, coming back from a trip to the park, Stephanie told Michael that she was his sister and that they had the same dad, but that dad had died.

Michael was so happy and excited by this news; now he had a sister and two dads, wow! Rod was so relieved by this as he had felt Michael may reject him.

That December, John and I visited Malaysia, another country John had already been with his late wife Val. I was anxious to visit

Melaka as that town had just been added to the new geography syllabus. We flew into Kuala Lumpur, visiting Merdeka Square with its lovely colonial buildings and the beautiful Hindu temple as well as Lake Gardens with its wonderful bird park, where you can walk through a huge aviary, and shopping at the central and night markets.

Then we rode a bus to Melaka, where the historic city centre was even more impressive as the Dutch-built colonial buildings had been painted crimson by the British when they colonised the region. The huge Christ Church, where I decided to do Christmas mass, and the clock tower were also red, so it really was a red square, far from Russia. The city's historic centre achieved UNESCO World Heritage status in 2008. I visited the information centre, mentioning that the city had been added to the NSW education syllabus and was given several pamphlets and a rather special plaque of the Malacca Sultanate Palace, which at that stage I hadn't found.

We then took a six-hour bus ride up into the Cameron Highlands, seeking respite from the thirty plus temperatures, and stayed at a tea plantation recommended in Lonely Planet. It was nice to just sleep, eat and rest in the cool for two days before we were back on a bus to Georgetown. Normally, I would say I much prefer the countryside to towns, but the cities in Malaysia were amazing.

The historic centre of George Town, on the island of Penang, also achieved UNESCO World Heritage status in 2008, together with Malacca.

The magnificent mansions of Chinese merchants have been restored and, together with the Taoist temple and an Indian-influenced mosque, reflect the distinctly different cultures who made this town.

John was so looking forward to the two-hour ferry trip to the island of Langkawi; I don't think he had been so long without a trip to the beach. Langkawi certainly lived up to its reputation, perfect beach and delicious seafood restaurant. Two days of sleeping, sunning, splashing and eating.

Back to George Town and on to Kota Bharu, a seven-hour bus trip. John had been here previously, but I wasn't impressed.

The beach wasn't as nice as Langkawi, and I was ready for more sightseeing rather than sunbathing. Finally, the monsoon weather arrived, so instead of proceeding to Kuala Terengganu, we caught the bus back to Kuala Lumpur, spending a few extra days before our flight home.

That year also, having the prospect of a hip replacement, I reluctantly sold Sangria. From the time of his birth, I had handled him, stoking, brushing, feeding him titbits. His mother came when I called, so he came to and became accustomed to the strange things I would do to him like putting on a halter, which he immediately tried to dislodge by rearing and swiping at it, then rolling, trying to rub it off. After many times, he finally accepted it. Then I tried lunging him, having his halter attached to a long rein, which I held, and then sent him trotting around me in a circle. This he adapted to very quickly. I was fulfilling a childhood dream; having bred a foal, I was going to break him in. I had him castrated while he was still with his mother for her to comfort him.

The other bay mare also had a colt, and when the time came to wean them, they were company for each other. They were left in the foaling paddock while both mums were removed and an elderly gelding installed to teach them manners. This was where I learned that young horses, when being bossed around by an older horse, would show their teeth, as if to say, 'I am only a baby. Don't punish me'. When I brought Chianti back to the riding school to enable the weaning, I discovered she hadn't really lost her mummy width, and I was finding it painful to ride her as I couldn't seem to stretch my hips wide enough to encompass her girth. When I went to the doctor, I was diagnosed with degenerative arthritis in the right hip and told that I could try physiotherapy, but eventually that I would need a hip replacement, and that would mean an end to horse riding.

That was the day my horse-riding dream died. I would not be able to train Sangria to do wonderful things. I could not even expect to take Chianti to the next level in dressage. At a horse show near Windsor, I had seen this very elderly lady competing on a beautiful black thoroughbred, doing dressage to music. My two loves combined! I was instantly inspired to do this with Chianti now and Sangria in the future. But it was not to be.

First, I had to have Sangria broken in as I would not be doing that myself anymore. He was now four years old as I hadn't wanted him to be broken in earlier.

I sent him to a race horse trainer living nearby, where Simone had sent the other foal the year before. He was a lovely, soft-spoken man who fed his horses only the best feed, didn't race two-year-olds and insisted the horses had a quiet siesta each day, closing the main door to the stable block, pulling the shades and playing quiet classical music to rest by. When I told him I would have to sell Sangria as I couldn't ride anymore, he told me to get the prospective buyer to spend an afternoon with him and Sangria, and he would instruct them as well. The last day of Sangria's instruction, Simone came with me and rode him as I looked on with tears in my eyes, knowing my horse-riding days were over. Then Simone rode over and said,

'Here, have a go. He is relaxed and at home, so he shouldn't startle and throw you'.

I needed a mounting stool to get on; he had grown so tall, taller than his mum, I realised, but not as broad, so stretching my hips was easier. I rode around the arena, savouring his long, easy stride, and then tried a trot, but that was more painful for me, so I sat and eased into a canter. For just five minutes, I felt transported in ecstasy, riding the horse I had bred, had seen born, had handled since birth and now was so responsive to my command. Then it was time to leave and bring Sangria home for the last time.

So I advertised, knocked back one unsuitable applicant and then instantly took a liking to a lovely young girl, who was quite happy to have a lesson with Sangria, before she took him home. As luck would have it, Sangria was going to live in Terrey Hills, only half an hour away from Manly Vale, and I could come and see him anytime. I only went once to see him comfortably settled in a stable with yard attached, in a complex of eight stables, all rented by girls riding in the bushland behind and planning to go to the St. Ives Show. Once

I was happy that Sangria had found a wonderful home, I did not follow his journey as one can never tell what the future may hold.

Chianti was another story. She was now fourteen, and I was too attached to her to ever consider selling. I visited once a month just to brush and be with her, often taking the children or grandchildren of friends to have a horse-riding lesson. Once a teacher, always a teacher. Chianti was very obliging; motherhood or age had settled her temperament, and she would walk, trot and canter on demand. This continued for eighteen years when one summer morning, I had a phone call from Simone to say Chianti was lying down and would not come to get her breakfast, so she was going to call the vet. He duly came and said her blood pressure was very low, and as the temperature was going to pass thirty that day, he felt her time had come, and he would give her a lethal injection. So she died peacefully, surrounded by people who loved her. Paul, Simone's husband, cut a length of her mane, which Simone plaited and gave to me when I visited. Such a thoughtful gift, so now I had a ribbon from Frenchs Forest Show, a rosette from Northside Riding Club dressage competition, a plait and many, many photos and memories to treasure.

John and I continued our yearly travels to Thailand, India and, our most adventurous of all, Africa.

CHAPTER 50

1995 – On Safari in Africa

I HAD READ AN advertisement for a month-long trip to Central Africa, including a safari in the Masai Mara, Kenya, and a trip to visit the mountain gorillas in the Congo. As the flight required change of plane in Harare, Zimbabwe, we decided to have a week in that country to see the Victoria Falls. First a visit to the National Gallery in Harare, walking along a pleasant boulevard lined with flowering trees. My Lonely Planet guide said this was like an Australian state capital and was a safe place to walk about; therefore, I was somewhat surprised to find two well-dressed young African males suddenly right in front of me, blocking my path. I had not noticed John had fallen behind, speaking to a third well-dressed African man. Then I felt a hand on my bag, which I wore around my waist. My reaction amazed and frightened me.

Grabbing his wrists, I screamed into his face,

'Don't you dare touch me'.

He dropped the wallet he had already removed from my bag, and it fell, scattering my credit card and coins. Instinctively, I bent down to collect my stuff, while the three Africans ran up the street, John hollering in hot pursuit.

No harm done, except to my state of mind, as I realised what a dangerous situation my reaction might have caused. If anyone would have asked me, what would you do in such condition, I would have said,

'Here, take my money. Just don't hurt me'.

My reaction of confronting him could have led to being attacked physically, and by bending down to pick up my stuff, I left myself open to attack, especially as there were three of them. One had asked John the time, which was why he had paused, and two blocked my path. It took many weeks before I felt confident walking the streets again without the need to hold John's hand.

My state of mind was not improved by our introduction to Nairobi when we landed in Kenya. We had the name of the hotel the tour would leave from, so we took one of the black English-type taxis that were lined up at the airport. It must have been approaching 6pm, and the streets were full of cars and people. As the taxi stopped at a red light, several people would rush to the taxi, dragging the window down, reaching in and demanding money. I huddled into John, both of us on the far side of the seat, away from the encroaching hands, while the driver sat impassively, staring ahead, not saying a word. I think I was ready to give up on our African adventure by the time we reached our hotel and just go home. The next morning, the news was not good. The tour operator wanted us to visit his office that day as there was a problem with the trip. When we questioned the hotel staff about how far his office was and were told we needed to go by taxi, I was ready to say, 'Let's call the whole thing off'. However, the hotel staff assured us that if we caught a local taxi just like the ordinary blue car waiting outside, we would not have a problem. She explained that the black English taxis were owned by a member of parliament and dominated the tourist trade, being the only ones allowed at the airport and at the main hotels in the centre of the city, and people objected to this monopoly. So we happily caught the blue taxi and arrived at the travel agency without any problem.

Here the news was quite devastating. The business was in difficulty, having been unable to access money paid by English and Australian clients. There had not been sufficient people to cover the cost of the originally planned tour, and what they were proposing as a variation to the original month-long tour was a fourteen-day trip to visit the gorillas, a seven-day trip to the Masai Mara and a four-day visit to Amboseli. We would lose three days but would have two personalised trips with just us attending. John was annoyed about paying more for personalised trips as he preferred meeting new people. I was so relieved that at least we would still be seeing the mountain gorillas, which, to me, were the main attraction; and as we had both come so far, we accepted.

The trip to Amboseli was first, with the towering Mt Kilimanjaro behind sweeping plains with wildebeests, zebra and massive herds of elephants, which, it seemed to me, had really damaged the environment as there were few trees, whose leaves were not stripped to the height of an elephant's tusk. Our guide told us that there was a problem with poachers, who killed the animals to take the ivory tusks. This guide set up our tent, supplied our bedding, cooked our food and heated water for us to wash, and he slept under the jeep. A side visit to Tsavo National Park, and then we were off to visit the gorillas, this time as a group of seven aboard the secondary vehicle, as the main one was still unavailable.

What an interesting group of people they were; I thought David Williamson would have made a wonderful play about our characters and our exploits. Three females other than me. A recently divorced lady from Double Bay, Sydney, on safari in Africa, while her ex-husband took their young children skiing in Switzerland. Dressed in spotless white linen pants and flowing top, she had a huge suitcase, which took two males to lift on to the top of the vehicle, as she had bought her own sheets and pillow to feel at home while camping. Next, a young white South African lady, who, I envisaged, had fought her way to the top of her profession, discarding lesser beings in her wake. She had the most unfortunate South African superior accent, and when she said 'driver', which she did regularly, it really put my teeth on edge with its arrogant tone. The third, a very quiet, efficient New Zealand nurse, whose fluent French conversation with the guards eased our crossing into Zaire. Her husband was a very talkative advertising executive. He literally had verbal diarrhoea and was quite funny for the first few moments, and then I would silently scream but didn't say, 'Shut up!' Finally, an older man from the USA, who had been everywhere, had done everything and was anxious to tell you everything you didn't know. Our driver, Bill, was a young Englishman who had been driving buses of eighteen- to thirty-five-year-olds on safari. This was an older, more affluent clientele, and he had no hope of controlling them.

The vehicle was a very tired army-type jeep with seating for seven and good views from the windows. We were only three days into our journey when it first overheated, necessitating carrying a large bottle of water and regular stops and cooling-off periods. This was fine as our first destination was the Masai Mara, where there were plenty of occasions to stop and look at copulating lions, cheetahs enjoying a kill, buffalo, wildebeests, hyena, giraffes and herds of elephants. One late afternoon, we even managed to see a leopard calmly making its way past a line-up of observing cars. Bill was very good at spotting, so we had a fulfilling safari. However, the car was a real problem. Once we had to lose most of the day to have a spring repaired by a local village mechanic. Then it refused to start in the morning without a push or tow. Once we had stopped to watch a lioness with two cubs playing and trying to climb the tree, their mother rested under. Inadvertently, Bill turned the motor off, so we had to wait until the lioness decided to leave before we could get out and push our car. Because we had lost so much time, Bill decided to cross Lake Victoria by boat instead of driving around, and into Uganda, where tanks left behind by the recent war were abandoned everywhere, then across Zaire and into Congo. I must mention here that our trip to Africa was in 1995 when the French-colonised country of Zaire still existed. In 1997, it combined with Congo.

Virunga National Park, the home of the mountain gorillas, lies on the border of two countries: Congo and Rwanda.

We camped at the base of the mountain, next to a village, whose members came and danced and sang for us that evening. Instructions for visiting the national park were very strict. We were checked out by medical staff from the village; no coughs, colds or fevers would be permitted to enter. Only six people at a time could visit the gorillas, so five of our group, plus guide, would visit one family group, and John and I, with a couple from Rwanda, would visit the other. Because we were considered to be slow of foot, we had to leave before daybreak with a guide to get there in time. Thank goodness I had packed a torch, raincoat and nuts for instant energy. We walked past the village, through their fields of crops, up and up the mountain side, till we reached the park office, just as the first rays of sun were appearing. Another safety briefing: Don't run. Only whisper. Don't try to touch the gorillas! As if we were likely to be close enough to do that, I thought. Led by two guides, one with a machete and one with a rifle, we fought our way through the jungle for what seemed like ages until we stopped, and the guide pointed out the nests in the trees where the gorillas had spent the night. Now we would follow their trail until almost high noon, we entered a clearing and found a family resting, the females grooming each other while the big silverback raised his head and stared at us. The youngsters in the trees, however, continued to swing and dive, one landing within reaching distance of our group. Another one had landed on the other side of our group and literally pushed his way in to join his mum. I felt so privileged to spend time observing their family dynamics. Walking back through the rain, I was so grateful to John for happily joining me on this adventure. I certainly would not have braved Africa without him.

We were lucky to meet our family at rest time. The others had to run to keep up with their group as they were moving at a rapid pace, feeding as they went. That trip was the highlight for me, but for others, the best was yet to come: the Ngorongoro Crater in Tanzania. An incredible twenty-kilometre-wide volcanic crater with six-hundred-metre walls, packed with just about every species of wildlife to be found in East Africa as there is permanent water and pasture. The Masai tribespeople live there also, grazing their cattle, fiercely protecting them from lions. We drove down into the crater, seeing hundreds of flamingos wading in the soda lake at the bottom, and followed the road along some way, meeting lots of other animals. Then disaster struck; our vehicle just stopped and refused to go any farther. We might be in the most populous park in Africa but had to get out of the car as nature called. How lucky are guys to just stand and relieve themselves? We ladies went looking for any sort of bush or depression to hide, but none appeared, so two of us held out a sarong as part protection. Our Double Bay lady, who was looking quite dishevelled by this time, just laughed and took her turn. With the hood raised, we had several people offer assistance, but the vehicle refused to cooperate. Finally, the park ranger appeared in a truck, which took us and our luggage back to the national park rest house at Momella. First, he had to make a detour, and driving across the grassland instead of on the road, we came across a mother rhino and newborn calf. He had to take photos of it without upsetting the mum, which was no easy task and one we eagerly watched. It was almost worth the inconvenience of travelling by truck to our next lodging to have witnessed this.

The following day, a charter bus arrived to take us back to Nairobi, where we were given $100 each and asked to sign a form stating we would not tell the story to others. As that is now twenty-seven years ago, and I have not named the company (if it still exists), I guess I am off the hook.

CHAPTER 51

1997 — Farewell, Avalon; Hello, Mrs Morgan

THE YEAR 1997 WAS when Sandra married Greg and then had Ethan, a mate for Brenton. The previous year, my niece Debbie had married Latham, later producing Connor and Kaleb.

Also, in 1997, my tenants came into an inheritance and wanted to buy my house. I was thrilled for them, as to me, they were the perfect owners, with two little boys, a baby girl and a dog. So I had the house valued and said I would sell it to them for that valuation price without going through a real estate agent. However, that third child caused a problem with getting a mortgage, so they tried another financial outlet and admitted to having only two children. When the assessor came to check out the house, they had removed all signs of the baby, and I was there, doing the owner inspection and vouching for their two-child situation. My little bedsit in Mona Vale had not been able to accommodate all my house furniture, so I had only taken one single bed, one chest of drawers and the TV with stand there, leaving the rest of my furniture in the house and including it in the sale price.

Having finalised the sale of Avalon, I went looking at units for sale in the Manly region, thinking $300,000 would only manage to buy a unit in this area. It is very difficult to adapt to unit living when you have always lived in a house. I saw many properties, units and town houses in good locations but always felt they were not quite right for me. Then I looked at a little cottage in Manly Vale, right next door to St Kieran's Primary School. It had been built back in the forties, originally on a large block of land, but recently that had been subdivided, with a small brick house and attached garage behind. The front house was fibro, clad to look like weatherboard, with a tiny enclosed front and back garden and a carport separating it from the neighbour behind. Just perfect, I thought, and happily took out a mortgage for the extra fifteen thousand it cost. Tenants were already living there, so I continued their lease as that would help repay the mortgage as I continued to live with and look after John. The threat of a hip replacement didn't eventuate until 2006 as I had persevered with physiotherapy, aqua aerobics and various herbal treatments to keep the pain away. When it became too painful to ignore, I had the operation while still living in John's two-storey house. I was unable to manage the stairs, so I slept on the downstairs lounge and used the shower of the tenant in the connecting flat. Very quickly, I realised I would probably have to have the other hip replaced and wanted to be in my own single-storey house when this happened. When my long-term tenants wanted to buy my Avalon house, Paul, Karen's husband, took the time to completely renovate my house, adding front and back porches with just two steps each and removing uneven surfaces within the house. All this was achieved in 2010, ready well before my second operation in 2012.

In 1998, when my mother turned eighty, I organised a party held on a boat trip on the lake and invited her entire family. All her children and grandchildren were there, except Nancye, Andy, Stephanie, Jacob and Amber, who couldn't be there that weekend but visited a week later when we had a second birthday cake. Leeanne and Rod, with Michael, Brandon and Kurt, drove to Forster to attend her birthday and decided to get married that day, so there was a double celebration. Actually, it was a triple celebration as I had confided to my sister that I felt a need to be married before I moved into my new house, but still, I was totally surprised when the third toast of the day was to John and me and our forthcoming nuptials.

The next wedding celebration was to be my own. Strangely, although I had been happy to live in John's house to take care of him while he recuperated from his triple bypass and happy to stay on when that shared care for each other became something more, I did not want to continue that relationship in my house. Possibly, the effects of two overseas holidays, with different names on our passports, had an influence, and although I had considered myself a liberated female from a young age, I was still a product of my era, the forties; and suddenly, I was wanting a white picket fence (which my new house had) and stable married life. So as a liberated female, I told my lover I needed him to marry me if he wanted to live in my house. John, uncomprehending this new attitude, but ever willing to do whatever was necessary to keep me happy, agreed and suggested we could honeymoon in Hawaii as he had bought a timeshare unit there years ago and really wanted to get rid of it. It had served as a wedding present to his granddaughter, and he didn't think the others would want a similar gift, so we could make a trip there, and then he could sell.

We used the marriage celebrant who had officiated at a nudist wedding held at Cobblers Beach which John and I had attended. Because we were going to Hawaii for our honeymoon, it seemed appropriate to hold the ceremony at Harbord Diggers Club, where there was an imposing statue of Duke Kahanamoku gracing the front entrance. We had been members for some years, so there was no problem booking a room and organizing a menu. Invitations were sent, requesting that no presents be bought (as we already had two households of married goods), but guests would be asked to pay for their meal in little red envelopes (as in the Chinese tradition of giving money and good luck). Fortunately, enough money was raised this way to cover the bill, plus a tip! My friend Ann made the cake, and her friend iced and decorated it with fresh flowers. All our respective families came, including Reg's three girls and offspring, and our special friends, and it was a lovely occasion with one little hiccup.

The celebrant had asked each of us to say I do to vows I had written and then turned to the audience to announce,

'I now pronounce you husband and wife'.

Somewhat astonished, I asked, 'Don't I get a ring?'

We had shopped for my wedding ring, which I knew John had in his blazer pocket. However, in our very friendly chat on the first meeting with the celebrant, John was very jovial about the wedding plans. I don't think he had really adjusted to the fact that this was actually happening. When rings were mentioned, he just joked,

'Well, we already have some of those', so the celebrant thought we weren't bothering with rings. As she assumed we belonged to the nudist crowd, who were somewhat unpredictable in habits, she didn't question.

This change in procedure quite amused John's son Ian, who said loudly,

'Dad, have you lost the ring?'

The celebrant rapidly took control again and asked John to place the ring on my finger, and then I knew this marriage would last until death do us part.

We had three weeks in Hawaii, one staying in John's timeshare in Honolulu, one on the island of Maui and one on the Big Island. Our visit to the Big Island coincided with the Hula festival in Hilo, and we also visited the Hawaiian Volcano National Park and walked the Kilauea Caldera. Maui, of course, has the best surfing beaches, so John had to go there, but there was such a strong undertow in the water, I lost my two-week-old wedding ring!

Back to Honolulu, and for the three days prior to the flight home, I spent hunting for a new wedding ring. It was not an easy task as the fashion in Hawaii that year was for rings to be engraved, scrolls or patterns on them. On our last day before leaving, I found a plain gold band.

In the following year, when Sydney hosted the Olympics, John rented his house, and we flew to the home of the Olympics, Greece, visiting Turkey on the way. It was lovely to catch up with my old friend Trish, who lived on the isle of Corfu, and in Turkey, I was most impressed with the underground houses of Cappadocia.

CHAPTER 52

2002 – Surprise, Surprise

THIS WAS THE YEAR I decided to retire from teaching. I had started in 1962 and, with four years out to produce babies, had been fully committed for all those years. Another reason was the previous year, there had been great changes in the Education Department. There had been declining enrolments in public schools, especially high schools, and to meet this situation, closures were imminent. Manly Boys High was only saved by becoming a selective high school, Manly High, ensuring a stable population. Manly Girls High became Freshwater Senior High, smaller in size, having only fifth and sixth form, and Beacon Hill High was destined to close. I felt I should step down to open up a position for the librarian from the closing school. So at the end of term 3, I resigned. However, in September of that year, I had a phone call from someone from a London television show, *Surprise, Surprise*. I hadn't heard of it, so she explained that the show connected far-flung relatives who hadn't seen each other for years, and they were wanting to reunite my mother with her twin brother, whom she hadn't seen for fifty-four years!

My reply was that they would have to fly the brother here as my mother wouldn't get on a plane. I had offered to take her years ago, and she was adamant that she wouldn't fly.

'Well, I have just been speaking to your mum, and she is happy to fly and wants you to come with her' was her answer. John and I drove to Forster that weekend. I had rung her doctor's surgery to ask his advice as my mother had been in the hospital with pneumonia the previous December. He reiterated that she was frail, and it could possibly be a strain on her heart, for which she already wore patches. When I told my mother this, she said,

225

'Well, it is all arranged and paid for, and I am going, so I will ring him and tell him so'.

Which she did, and he responded by writing a letter for her to take, which said she needed a wheelchair and preferably a stopover to break the journey and could have oxygen supplied, if she needs it.

So I retired early, and on 4 December, Mum and I boarded the British Airways flight to Singapore. The day was very warm, and passengers needing assistance were the first to board, so we sat for a long time before take-off. Fortunately, the London clothes were in our luggage, so we were in summer dresses, and the airline staff bought Mum a glass of champagne when she told them she was going to be on *Surprise, Surprise*, which all of them had watched. My handbag was full of Mum's medication and puffers, a gentle tranquiliser before we left, anti-anxiety pill if needed on the flight and Ventolin for any shortness of breath. Fortunately, the flight was smooth; the only problem occurred when mum needed to go to the bathroom. She needed a walking stick and also needed to hang onto chairs as she passed. I was really concerned she would fall, but a cheery male attendant came up and said, 'You go in front, and I'll bring up the rear, and we will catch her whichever way she falls'. I was so grateful to him.

We only had one night in Singapore to rest, but Mum had never seen the city and was anxious to have a look, so with help from the hotel staff, who also treated her like a television star, we hired a trishaw to just see the town. Of course, Mum wanted to shop, and I said we couldn't because we didn't have the right money, but she could buy souvenirs at the airport.

By the time we reached London, we were both exhausted, and I was so glad that instead of providing a wheelchair which I would have to push, the staff came along with a motorised elderly passenger conveyer. Through customs and then by taxi to our hotel. Suddenly, one warm coat was not enough; I needed woollen socks and track pants. The wind was icy, not snowing, but definitely cold enough. How I wished the show had been made in the summer months. We had a day to recover. Fortunately, the hotel had a souvenir shop for

Mum to shop, so we didn't have to venture out. I was still worried about my mother's recent bout of pneumonia and if it would recur.

Monday morning, we were taken to the recording studio for rehearsal. Mum had already been advised that she should wear solid colours, no stripes, plaid or geometric patterns, so she was wearing a new rich blue dress we had bought that first weekend I visited when the winter sales were on. There was no Cilla Black, the presenter, and no brother Jack; he was still unaware this was happening. Only the film crew and producer were there, organising where to stand and move on stage. Mum had to stand in the wings while a stand-in Jack was presented to a stand-in Cilla. Then, on a cue, given by a man in the wings, mum had to walk on stage and give her best beaming smile to those there. I insisted mum needed a chair to sit on while she waited, as I thought she might collapse from the suspense. After perfecting the walk-on, we went to the dining room for dinner, followed by the contestants being sent to the green room to await the show.

To explain how this all came to pass, Jack's daughter, Brenda, had a daughter, Kerry, and they were regular watchers of the show. When Jack's eightieth birthday was approaching, Kerry wrote to say that she would dearly like to reunite her grandfather with his twin sister, whom he hadn't seen in over fifty years. The team visited Jack and his wife, Flo, and all their close neighbours, doing a survey of family relationships. They told the participants that the reward for one lucky couple would be a night out to a show in London. They interviewed Brenda, her husband and Kerry, noting the posters she had on her wall, and then informed them that they would be going to the show with her mum and dad.

Of course, I had bought presents for all my British relatives as it was so close to Xmas, but how did an opal pendant stack up against an all-expenses-paid trip to London? While we were in the green room, we met the other contestants. One girl was being reunited with a mother who had given her up for adoption when she had been an unmarried teenager. Another girl was being reunited with her father, her mother having left him to seek a new life in Canada. This girl now had a husband and three little boys. The anticipation and emotion in that room was palpable. The adopted girl kept running to the toilet and the mother of three almost hysterical in corralling her sons.

I was able to go with Mum and wait in the wings when, on cue, she took a deep breath and, head held high, marched out to give the most dazzling smile to her brother. Then something I didn't expect happened as it hadn't been in our rehearsal. Cilla told Mum and Jack to go back to the green room to have a long talk, and she called Kerry to the stage.

'Now, young lady, I believe it was you who wrote and ask us to find your grandfather's twin sister. I believe you deserve a prize for that, and I know that you really like pop singer Gareth Gates, so I asked him for a cassette, but he thought I might keep it, so he decided to come along and give it to you himself'.

From the other side of the wings arrived the pop star in question, bearing a huge framed photo of himself, signed 'To Kerry, with love from Gareth Gates'. Then he put his arm around her, kissed her and proceeded to dedicate his latest song to her and sang it right at her. I no longer worried about the paucity of my present.

After the show, there were drinks and canapes, and Cilla met and had photos taken with all the participants. It was a simply amazing evening, and my mum was starry-eyed.

On the first conversation with the team, I had mentioned Mum would want to see her other brother, who lived in Skegness. A week before we were due to leave Australia, a very apologetic assistant rang to say that the only flight she could get us on was on Christmas Day. We would still stop over in Singapore, and in an apology for spoiling our Xmas, they would pay for Christmas dinner at the hotel! I knew Ian and Kirsty would take Owen to the club for Xmas dinner, so it was a win-win situation.

The bus trip to Skegness was quite an eye-opener for me. I didn't realise how narrow the country roads in England were or how they were all lined with huge hedges you couldn't see past. We spent a lovely week with Uncle Bun and his wife and their gorgeous little dog, and then it was back home to Australia.

Back in Australia, we received the devastating news that Cilla Black had left the network that ran *Surprise, Surprise*. The company had replaced her with a younger female in her other dating show, so she walked out of *Surprise, Surprise*, which was a top-rating show that had been hers from the start. So that very expensive broadcast, featuring two from Australia and a family of five from Canada, never went to air. We were sent a DVD of the recording.

CHAPTER 53

2006 – Shad Arrives

I CAN'T END MY story without a mention of the dogs that filled my life.

One day, while walking the Manly foreshore with John, I met Margaret, a girl I had known from line dancing, walking a little white dog. She told me he came from Monica's Doggie Rescue, Terrey Hills, where she volunteered once a week. I was so missing a dog, I decided to join her, and we took turns in driving there. We would cook kilos of donated chicken legs with carrots at home and then mix that with rice we cooked there and feed the fifty or so dogs with that mixture. At that stage, most of the dogs were small, and it wasn't long before one in particular caught my eye, being so terrified and in need of a permanent home. This was Victor, renamed Shad (short for Shadow as he never left my side), who came to live in Manly Vale. John installed fencing to enclose the backyard, but Shad never strayed. Being white and fluffy, he needed to be clipped, but I was not confident to do it myself, so I took him to the local groomer, who was only able to do very little, saying she thought that he might lose an eye if she continued and that he needed to be clipped under sedation. At first, I took him to the vet, where he was sedated and then unceremoniously shorn. The result was not a pretty sight!

Then Katherine, a girl who had been grooming dogs at Monica's, told me she was opening her own business in Brookvale, and if I wanted to bring Shad along the day before the business opened officially, she would spend time to accustom him to grooming. At first, she would give him a very light sedative and a bath and try a little clip, backing off when he became too anxious. With regular trips, he became used to the procedure, and sedation was no longer necessary.

Three years later, I had a call from my friend Peter's daughter, Lauren, saying she had to give up her puppy as the new accommodation wouldn't allow a dog. That was when Patsy joined our family and became a special pal of Shad. The two lived in harmony for many years. Shad was the first to go, aged seventeen, and Patsy followed three years later when she was fifteen. Both wonderfully loyal pets to the end.

In 2008, John and I embarked on an Evergreen Tour, which started as a Danube River cruise, from Amsterdam to Budapest, and then by bus to Warsaw. We were having a wonderful time when a telephone call from Australia announced my mother had died. Ian's mother-in-law had rung every travel agent in Manly, Manly Vale and finally Balgowlah, where she found our agent and relayed the news. The staff on the ship were wonderful and organised a return flight to Sydney from the city of Budapest, which was our next port of call. I came home, drove to Forster and gave my mother's eulogy, announcing the family secret of my mother's first love that had been hidden all my siblings' lives.

In 2001, to celebrate my eightieth birthday, the girls planned to take me to Outback Spectacular as the show had a particularly appropriate storyline about the young couple Maureen and Reg, the difficulties on the farm and the appearance of a wild horse.

Something I would like to share before I end this story, I am now a great-grandmother to three, with Stephanie marrying Scott and producing Chase, Aidan and Lily, and also a step-great-grandmother to thirteen, with Karen's daughter Jesse finding Matt and producing Jordan, Siobhan and Adelaide; her brother Matt marrying Jesse, producing Jayden and Hamish; and her sister Alicia marrying James, having Hudson. Vicky's daughter Caitlyn had a daughter, Delaney; Lee Morgan's elder son, Tim, married Nicole, having Camilla, Flo-Jo, Henry and Lucette; and the younger son, Chris, married Lucy, having Eliza and Isabelle.

A strange symmetry has surrounded my life. My elder child, Michael, was born on 27 October, exactly three weeks and one day before my birthday, 18 November. My younger son, Greg, was born on 3 December, exactly three weeks and one day after mine, and three weeks and one day later is Christmas Day. I also have had a strange affinity with the number 11 most of my adult life. I was married in 1966, l left my husband in 1977, and I moved in with John in 1988 and married him in 1999. I had thought I would be widowed in 2011, but John survived until 2013. Having thought about this story back in 2008, I thought I had better have it finished early in 2022.

Content Group UK Ltd.
s UK
0323
377/J